Deciding for Ourselves is the perfect book for our times. Each essay traces the possibilities (and even offers up some road maps) for how to survive our current situation with dignity and autonomy. The essays, beautifully curated by Cindy Milstein, point to a nuanced version of direct democracy that isn't just a utopian idea but instead something that is already happening amid our complex social systems. Read this exciting book with your friends and community for inspiration and hope, and then get busy enacting radical social change together!

CARLA BERGMAN, coauthor of *Joyful Militancy:*
Building Thriving Resistance in Toxic Times

We urgently need *Deciding for Ourselves* right now. As conditions of wealth concentration, state violence, social isolation, and climate crisis accelerate, more and more people are trying to figure out new ways of being together, meeting basic needs, and fighting back. To build the sustained mutual aid and vibrant resistance that these times demand, we need to study what people all over are learning about making decisions together under pressure and creating flexible yet durable ways of self-organizing. This anthology provides detailed, wonderfully useful accounts of on-the-ground experiences of seizing space and making power.

DEAN SPADE, author of *Normal Life: Administrative*
Violence, Critical Trans Politics, and the Limits of Law

This wonderful book feels like a lively late-night conversation with just the kinds of people you most want to be talking to, leaning forward over plates of food and mugs of wine, coffee, and tea to share these true stories, accounts of creative, compassionate, and generous communities, self-reflective, fluid, hardworking,

PRAISE FOR *DECIDING FOR OURSELVES*

scrupulously practical, and wildly dreamy. We talk deep into the night. We can't sleep! The stories keep coming! We look deep into each other's eyes across time and space. Tell me more. Let's make more of these stories come true together!

MADELINE FFITCH, author of *Stay and Fight: A Novel*

Deciding for Ourselves: The Promise of Direct Democracy represents what we need more of: the collective. Considering the promise of what's already been offered allows us to both imagine and implement new possibilities. That's why texts like this one are important. We can't neglect the significance of our ability to organize, whether that happens in person or on paper. This anthology is about what we can do, and there's enough perspective here to help us see that we have firm examples of inspiration already around us.

WILLIAM C. ANDERSON, coauthor of *As Black as Resistance: Finding the Conditions for Liberation*

This collection of essays, curated by Cindy Milstein with author/militants from around the globe, mightily contributes to an understanding of how we might create and live in a liberatory world. A must read for all who dream of and work for collective liberation.

ROXANNE DUNBAR-ORTIZ, author of *An Indigenous Peoples' History of the United States*

In fraught times, it is often hard to imagine, let alone build, real revolutionary possibilities. Far too many retreat or quail. Democracy is a complicated and treacherous idea, and direct democracy even more so. This collection is a drink of cool water on a hot day, a sweet break in the gloom, a shot of good coffee, a jump of adrenaline that suggests something else really is possible. It's a lovely set of stories that really does help to "sweep away the state inside us." Totally recommended.

MATT HERN, author of *What a City Is For: Remaking the Politics of Displacement*

Deciding fo

Ourselves

EDITED BY CINDY MILSTEIN

Deciding for Ourselves

THE PROMISE OF DIRECT DEMOCRACY

AK Press

Deciding for Ourselves: The Promise of Direct Democracy
Edited by Cindy Milstein
All essays © 2020 by their respective authors
This edition © 2020 AK Press (Chico, Edinburgh)
ISBN: 978-1-84935-373-1
EBOOK ISBN: 978-1-84935-374-8
Library of Congress Control Number: 2019947436

AK Press	AK Press UK
370 Ryan Avenue #100	33 Tower Street
Chico, CA 95973 USA	Edinburgh EH6 7BN Scotland
www.akpress.org	www.akuk.com

The above addresses would be delighted to provide you with the latest AK Press distribution catalog, which features books, pamphlets, zines, and stylish apparel published and/or distributed by AK Press. Alternatively, visit our websites for the complete catalog, latest news, and secure ordering.

Cover and interior design by Crisis
Cover photo by Simón Sedillo
Printed in Michigan on acid-free, recycled paper

TO ANDREW ZONNEVELD, without whom this anthology wouldn't have been possible; TO MURRAY BOOKCHIN, friend and mentor, who infused anarchism with a directly democratic ethos; AND TO ALL who still believe in and struggle to sustain the promise of collective freedom, righteous dignity, and rebellious love

Cindy Milstein

PRELUDE: DECIDING FOR OURSELVES

On the bleak terrain of a gray city,
Gray with misery & memories of death,
Where invisible hands devise "natural" disasters,
Constructing levees that break in hurricanes &
Nuclear power plants that melt in earthquakes,
While other invisible hands steal land & erect prisons,
Or shutter factories & schools,
While still more invisible hands privatize water,
Piling devastation on poor & marginalized people,
Black, Indigenous, female, queer, disabled, non-English speaking,
Anyone who is "other,"
The haggard rainbow of humanity,
Thrown out like so much trash
Into a landfill of socially constructed sorrows—
No one ever took credit,
But one morning, chalked on the sidewalk,
A message appeared:
"Meet here at 7:30 p.m."[1]

---

1. I originally wrote this piece as my part of a picture-essay in Cindy Milstein and Erik Ruin, *Paths toward Utopia: Graphic Explorations of Everyday Anarchism* (Oakland, CA: PM Press, 2012), 74–85. It was loosely based on an anecdote told by a participant in the popular rebellion that occurred in Argentina in 2001–2.

She rubbed the sleep from her eyes
To stare at the neatly printed words,
Here on her street corner.

The letters weren't there yesterday.
She was sure of it.
Every day, on her way to work,
This slab of pavement was her bus stop.

She always looked down,
Waiting silently among strangers,
Memorizing the gray concrete patch,
Then silently riding to her gray office.

"They've shut all the banks!"
A frantic voice exclaimed behind her.
She rubbed her eyes again & then widened them
The bus pulled up, wheezing to a halt.

"Come on, let's go downtown.
I hear people are smashing ATMs!"
This stranger, her neighbor who never said hello, smiled.
The driver smiled too: "No charge today."

The city was in pieces.
A financial collapse, it was said,
Based on fears of an ecological collapse.
She knew the metropole was already in tatters.
In her neighborhood, there was plenty of nothing.

At 7:30 p.m., every one of her neighbors,
People who never gave each other the time of day,
Filled the usually empty intersection.
No one ever knew how,
But that night, an assembly was birthed.

At first men spoke more often, because patriarchy wasn't gone.
Soon, though, women & other genders demanded to be heard.
White people interrupted brown ones, because racism wasn't gone.
Soon people of many colors demanded to be respected.
Nearly everyone wanted to exert control, because hierarchy wasn't gone,
Because they were all born into a world of states & capitalism &
    oppression.
Soon people learned, through trial & error, how to listen.
They also learned how to dialogue,
How to resolve conflict & problem solve.
Slowly, they learned how to decide for themselves.

Someone suggested they meet every evening.
Another person proposed that anyone, even kids, could participate.
Hands went up & heads nodded.
Yet they were unsure how to affirm decisions.
So they debated until they stumbled on a process:
Full consensus on weighty issues but two-thirds on minor ones;
To vote, people must attend regularly & live in the neighborhood,
But yes, given that, everyone can decide;
Decisions will be written out & wheat pasted on public walls;
All agreements can be revisited, if needed, after careful thought.

Over time, people increasingly found common ground.

They came to know & trust each other, so decisions seemed easier.

The assembly became more efficient & meetings were shorter.

Working committees, accountable to the nightly body, were set up.

The neighborhood, the neighbors, came alive.

Other neighborhoods did the same.

No one ever recollected how,

But effortlessly, cooperation between districts emerged.

Across the bleak terrain of this gray neighborhood,

People were determined to supply what they needed,

Settling on interdependent, collective spaces as the means.

Those with doctoring & wellness skills created solidarity-not-charity clinics.

Those who knew how to run machines reopened factories, without bosses.

Children designed their own schools, picking their teachers & curriculum.

No one ever knew who painted them,

But soon, banners proclaiming victory appeared on lampposts:

"Para todos todo"

"Occupy everything"

"This is only the beginning"

Looking back, a few years later,

Long after her & her neighbors' assembly had fizzled out,

She wondered if it had been a dream.

No one ever grasped how,

But imperceptibly, "order" had been restored.

Financial markets & politicians took charge.

Hipster-pioneers migrated into the still-decimated city.

It hadn't been a total backslide; lovely remnants survived:
The collective theater troupe, squatting a former bank building,
A few of the block-by-block barter networks
& the hardy posse of free pedicabs.
Still, she wondered why many of her neighbors had abandoned self-
    governance,
Falling again under the sway of "comfortable," passive compliance.

One gray Monday at her bus stop,
Her neighbor who now always said hello
Paused before boarding to add,
"No one ever recalled how,
But one day, states were no longer natural or necessary.
It's not too early to reconvene our assembly.
What do you say?
Tonight at 7:30."

the Promise of Dignified Lives

Cindy Milstein

Imagine a sheet of ice covering a dark lake of possibilities. We scream "NO" so loud that the ice begins to crack. What is it that is covered? What is that dark liquid that (sometimes, not always) slowly or quickly bubbles up through the crack? We shall call it dignity.

—JOHN HOLLOWAY, *Crack Capitalism*, 2010

Ten years ago, when Holloway asserted "NO" as a way to start to break free, it still felt as if there were many "YES" stepping-stones on the journey toward social transformation. And a mere ten years before that, at the turn of the twenty-first century, our collective refusal and many affirmations offered an even clearer path, as the alter-globalization movement ran joyously through the streets proclaiming that "another world is possible."

Now, though, "NO" seems to have solidified into a bleak, fixed terrain. We are, one could argue, living in a time of no way out, no future, no hope. A deep foreboding that nothing good lies ahead has frozen us in our tracks. Despair hangs heavy, like a death shroud. Even our screams—whether of outrage, fear, or grief—appear unable to penetrate the icy heart of the current social order.

A large part of today's all-pervasive "NO" is the powerlessness we feel against the juggernauts of fascism and ecocide. These are formidable obstacles indeed. It is no small task to "crack" catastrophic climate shifts, much less the brutal authoritarianism sweeping the globe. It's easy to convince ourselves now that the end of the world is possible, or more accurately, that we humans are inevitably doomed, and perhaps soon, to extinction. How can we have hope in a world with increasingly diminished expectations for the future—or even *a* future? Or more to the point, what could it possibly mean to hang on to hope in an unprecedented time period, when there's no reliable magnetic pole to guide our compasses and thus navigate humanity out of harm's way?

"Hope," a dictionary will tell us, is about our ability "to cherish a desire with anticipation." The concept has a quality of expectation about it—an expectation, it should be added, that supplies a confidence or trust in the actual fulfillment of that cherished desire of ours. The word "trust," for its part, holds out a sense of "something future," and moreover, something entrusted to us to be cared for in that future. One could contend, and rightly so, that a hope without any hope of satisfaction is no hope at all. It's no wonder that people are feeling "despair," which if we consult our dictionary again, means "to lose hope utterly," giving up all expectation. Despair, in a nutshell, is a thoroughly normal reaction to all we're up against right now.

Yet we don't have to settle for a hope/despair binary. Life is always more complex, especially the inexact science of social relations and social organization. We could instead wander toward an observation made in 1958 by political philosopher Hannah Arendt in *The Human Condition* amid the mass carnage of National Socialism, Bolshevism, and Maoism, among others: "The remedy for unpredictability, for the chaotic uncertainty of the future, is contained in the faculty to make and keep promises," which depends on "the presence and acting of others."[1]

---

1. Hannah Arendt, *The Human Condition* (1958; repr., Chicago: University of Chicago Press, 2018), 237.

Diving again into our dictionary, we see that "promise" bespeaks a "pledge to do, bring about, or provide" something. With a promise, there is an implied ethical imperative. We don't have to make promises; we voluntarily decide to do so out of a sense of social goodness. From there, we depend not on top-down, legalistic, or external guarantees to make good on those promises—structures that ultimately necessitate coercive enforcement mechanisms; we rely on trust. Making a promise means giving each other our word. The assurance of that promise being kept resides in the strength of the face-to-face social fabric that we manage to cooperatively weave and sustain. We cocreate our own grounds for expectation—grounds that can only be cultivated and tended to by us. To put it modestly, as writer James Baldwin offered us in 1964, we promise and then demonstrate to each other that even if we "can't change the world always," we all have the capacity to do something "to make life a little more human."[2]

In 2020, then, against what seems a totalizing "NO," we could approach Holloway's dark lake from another angle. We could peer long and hard at the seemingly opaque sheet of ice in order to see the flickers of possibilities still swimming below the surface. We could notice the play of shadows darting about in the subterranean. We could and should remember that the impossible is still possible these days, even if only in small pools that freeze and thaw. The alternative is to accept oblivion. And that is no alternative at all.

On December 31, 2018, in a collective declaration of the "beginning of the war against oblivion," Subcomandante Insurgente Moisés observed,

---

2. James Baldwin, *The Cross of Redemption: Uncollected Writings* (New York: Vintage Books, 2011), 81.

It's easy to say, "we have to make the impossible possible," people say it all the time. But you have to actually do it in practice and this is what we are trying to show people. What is it that we are showing them? What we have before us: a people who govern themselves, with their own politics, their own ideology, their own culture. They create, improve, correct, imagine, and put it all into practice. This is what we are. Here the bad government does not rule; organized women and men rule. Those who are not organized will continue to rely on despair, because what they believe in is not actually hope.[3]

Moisés's words came on the eve of the twenty-fifth anniversary of the birth of the Zapatista autonomous communities. On New Year's Day 1994, there were "no universal recipes, lines, strategies, tactics, laws, rules, or slogans," as the Zapatistas put it, for what "good government" would look like in Chiapas, Mexico. Yet it was enough to know that bad governments had stolen lands and lives over many centuries. It was enough to know that people could experiment together, humbly self-organizing to improve their social conditions. It was enough to know, again to quote the Zapatistas, that there was "only a desire: to build a better world, that is, a new world," guided by principles such as to lead by obeying, construct not destroy, and work from below rather than seek to rise.[4]

---

3. "Words of the EZLN's CCRI-CG to the Zapatista Peoples on the 25th Anniversary of the Beginning of the War against Oblivion," Enlace Zapatista, January 9, 2019, accessed September 26, 2019, http://enlacezapatista.ezln.org.mx/2019/01/09/words-of-the-ezlns-ccri-cg-to-the-zapatista-peoples-on-the-25th-anniversary-of-the-beginning-of-the-war-against-oblivion/.

4. Clandestine Revolutionary Indigenous Committee, quoted in Luis Hernández Navarro, "Zapatismo Today and Tomorrow," January 16, 2004, accessed September 26, 2019, http://www.schoolsforchiapasr.org/wp-content/uploads/2014/06/Zapatismo-Today-and-Tomorrow-Understanding-the-Rebellion.pdf.

Two and a half decades later, fragile as this impossible possible self-governing region still is, it still is there. It is living proof that a wholly different society is doable, especially for those who've grown up in the autonomous communities, and come what may, it will remain a lodestar for other efforts. For as anarchist theorist Murray Bookchin observed, "If we do not do the impossible, we shall be faced with the unthinkable."[5]

So we have no choice but to venture bravely forth in this perilous time, hand in hand, promising we'll do our best, particularly under the worst of conditions, to love and care for each other. Indeed, we must redouble our efforts to alleviate as much suffering as we can while also emphasizing quality of life for the human and nonhuman world. As contributor Dilar Dirik indicates, we must "view revolution as a process that requires patience, care, [and] communality," striving toward "the development of life itself." And in order to make good on our mutual promises of dignified lives worth living in common, we must have the collective power to continually decide for ourselves.

This anthology holds out the promise of direct democracy. That promise is an incomparably beautiful balancing act between two forms of freedom: our grassroots institutions and cultures of self-governance, formal and informal, and our social relations of self-determination, in ethics and practice. Diverse forms of direct democracy offer us the best chance of creating the kinds of worlds we dream about because they allow us to determine together, dynamically over time, what we need and want in our own distinctive contexts. Yet we can only self-govern dreamily when we make and keep promises to each other, predicated on a commitment to social goodness

---

5. Murray Bookchin, *The Ecology of Freedom: The Emergence and Dissolution of Hierarchy* (Oakland, CA: AK Press, 2005), 107.

that is equally nurtured in how we treat each other on a regular basis, through all our joys and sorrows. *Deciding for Ourselves* uncovers what contributor Stefano Portelli calls "successful anarchism"—those spaces of self-organization from below that appear "almost spontaneously as soon as people figure out that they can free themselves from oppression and command," so that in turn, people can be who they fully aspire to become, and within humanly scaled communities that embrace them for the whole of their lives.[6]

This collection finds promise not in the abstract. Nor in doctrinaire formulas or easy answers. *Deciding for Ourselves* discovers it in the actual lived and still-living contemporary practices of what it means for people to govern themselves in urban and rural areas around the world as an implicit or explicit replacement for the state, whether neoliberal or fascist, and in the face of other infrastructures of death, like capitalism and patriarchy. The anthology's stories are not exhaustive, but they are fairly diverse. The book is a sampler—suggestive, inspiring, and nuanced—of how different peoples have set about structuring their own forms of self-governance based on their own experiences and contexts, undergirded by reciprocal promises of trust and solidarity. In this way, it unearths the substantively better circumstances that people create through their own collective power. As Yunuen Torres Ascencio puts it in contributor Scott Campbell's piece on the communal government in Cherán, Mexico, "'The *I* has become *us*' as a result of living in community."

Deciding for Ourselves also highlights that direct democracy must be custom-tailored by and for its participants—meaning no two places will

---

6. Stefano Portelli, email communication with me, December 2018.

look alike—or it can hardly be understood as self-governance; rather, it would be something designed or imposed from above. People may use different words, based on their languages and traditions, to describe how they decide for themselves, and those decisions may happen while chatting in a community garden, deliberating in a popular assembly, or solving conflicts in front of neighbors or at a workplace. But for those engaged in their own hybrid version of self-governance, such practices are a legible, recognized, and place-based part of their everyday lives.

None of the examples are the full or "right" answer, nor are they intended as blueprints. The pieces are each exactly that: pieces of the many parts of what makes direct democracy work, and that when combined, might perhaps begin to illuminate a wholistic understanding of a world without states. All the essays, though, gesture toward the notion that such spaces are not merely possible under the most difficult of present-day conditions—ranging from colonized lands to the gentrification of cities to fascistic war zones—but that they also bring forth the magic of heterogeneous forms of freedom. Thus this anthology explores the "sense of freedom in the air," as contributor Natasha King puts it, that can be found in these relatively long-lived and/or large-scale autonomous, directly democratic places. And while it doesn't shy away from the real-world dilemmas that these spaces must grapple with, it underscores the imaginative solutions, interdependent daily lives, and egalitarian sensibilities that are collectively generated in them, making the politics more than worth it.

For what is politics, at its heart, other than the question, Who gets to make the decisions that impact our lives, along with the life of our communities and the planet? Who has the ultimate power to decide, as our dictionary again offers, "the total complex of relations between people living in a society"? Throughout the history of social organization, there have only been three answers: sovereignty can be held by either the one, the few, or the many. Each of those replies has taken a variety of forms over the millennia, from the brutal tyrannies of the one, such as a despot or dictator, to the purportedly more progressive and humane few, such as aristocrats or elected representatives, to the always-existent common sense of the many determining their own lives for themselves via what contributor Modibo Kadalie describes as forms of "intimate direct democracy."

Yet with the rise and consolidation of the nation-state, with its parliaments and congresses, courts and cops, militaries and prisons, "seeing like a state," to borrow anthropologist James C. Scott's book title, became naturalized as the be-all and end-all of politics. With this shift toward politics-as-state, people were separated from, as Holloway depicts it, "the constant creation and re-creation of the[ir] community," to the point where now "the state separates people, separates leaders from masses, separates the political from the economic, the public from the private, and so on."[7]

Political theorist Raúl Zibechi, in looking at how contemporary movements are birthing new worlds by "dispersing power," maintains that "the most revolutionary thing we can do is strive to create new social relationships within our own territories—relationships that are born of the struggle, and are maintained and expanded by it." This voluntary task, in contrast to the coercive mechanisms of the state, daily commits us to "creating a new world to care for the people's power as the sacred fire of the movement. Let it beat in the heart of the people, a heart woven in popular sociability, without hierarchy or leaders."[8]

---

7. John Holloway, "Foreword to the German Edition," in *Dispersing Power: Social Movements as Anti-State Forces*, by Raúl Zibechi (Oakland, CA: AK Press, 2010), xvi.

8. Raúl Zibechi, *Dispersing Power: Social Movements as Anti-State Forces* (Oakland, CA: AK Press, 2010), 4, 7.

Or to put it another way, what anarchist Carlos Taibo calls the "direct democracy of equals" serves not only as a viable and ethical alternative for states or other forms of social domination; it gives us the breathing room to "seek to act as if we were free because, in so doing, we begin to be so."[9]

*

Through it all this past long-short almost two weeks, we've unfolded as people to each other. Not just what's nice and good about ourselves, but who we truly are, through fights and conflicts, misunderstandings and poorly stated comments during general assemblies, lack of skills and disorganization, sleeplessness and impatience.

I looked around this evening, at the many faces of people I didn't like at first, who I share little in common with, who I'd never in a million years be friends with. I looked around and realized that I like them. I am friends and/or friendly with them. Quirks and all. Because I'm starting to know their quirks, and goodness knows, they certainly know mine. We're turning into what people label "one big, happy family," where you know that means, "Yeah, your uncle kinda rambles on too long, but we love them anyway" or "Your cousin is a bit wild, but they're a good kid." And certainly that's true, with the fondness as well that underlies that sentiment of familiarity, of family you never asked for, but when push comes to shove, you're glad you have around.

More than that, though, we've turned into the stuff, on a micro level, of what might begin to feel like "one big, happy community," where our imperfections are what fondly bind us, allow us to make and keep promises, give us the desire to be there for and with each other, through thick and thin, without compulsion.

—CINDY MILSTEIN, *Outside the Circle* blog, fall 2011

---

9. Carlos Taibo, *Rethinking Anarchy: Direct Action, Autonomy, Self-Management*, trans. Autonomies Collective (Chico, CA: AK Press, 2019), 25, 35.

These words were written, in exhilarated sleeplessness, sometime between midnight and dawn, after barely fourteen days of what was called Occupy Philly.[10] Inspired by Occupy Wall Street, some thousand-plus people—most strangers to each other, and most not necessarily political—showed up about three weeks earlier for what was supposed to be a discussion in a modest-size, longtime anarchist bookstore, the Wooden Shoe. But before the event could even begin, it was clear that the crowd couldn't squeeze into the space. So someone managed to quickly convince a church to let us use its enormous sanctuary, and an anarchist friend and I started walking to the new location, about a mile away. We noticed that everyone was following us, in what became an impromptu and upbeat march en route, and that once at the church, people were looking to the small number of us anarchists to facilitate an organizing meeting.

A couple days later, after one more packed-church meeting, the thousand-plus people decided for themselves to squat the plaza encircling Philadelphia's city hall, despite us anarchists urging that we take more time to prepare. Based on our experience, we were skeptical that so many people new to self-organizing could suddenly, collectively and effectively, take and hold space. We were wrong. Within about twenty-four hours of occupying the barren concrete square, a vibrant city within a city had sprung up, with a directly democratic general assembly, numerous working groups, hundreds of tents including ones especially for the unhoused residents previously sleeping on this plaza, and an abundance of what people needed

---

10. All quotations from my blog, here and below, are pulled from numerous posts written during my participation in both Occupy Philly and the Quebec student strike. See the sections "Dispatches from Occupy Philly" and "Dispatches from Quebec Spring" at *Outside the Circle*, cbmilstein.wordpress.com.

and desired, from a library and kids' zone, to a community kitchen and medical aid, to indie media and DIY cultural events, to art and education spaces, to a tech area and a public living room complete with a couch, to trash collection and recycling, and so much more. In fact, people created more public infrastructure within Occupy Philly, in a matter of days, than the city of Philadelphia provided them on a regular basis.

On day three of Occupy Philly, I noted the "messy joy of watching thousands of people discover their own power," that they don't need "someone to compel, force, or boss them," and that "even if it's only temporary: self-organization works." Yet during that evening's general assembly, in the midst of painful "embryonic learning" over whether cops are good or not, I impatiently grumbled on my blog that "socialization is strong, from racism and heteronormativity to conceiving of 'politics' as a series of requests to those in power." I muttered under my breath, "How can these spaces offer so much promise, so quickly, and so quickly fall apart?" A mere two days later, on day five,

our evening general assembly seemed to suddenly recognize its own self-constituted power, and seemed to suddenly be adamant about using and preserving it. We grappled with a really tough, divisive proposal from the day before, related to whether we wanted a police liaison. It was a question of transparency, accountability, and us determining, as a general assembly, when and if we wanted to talk to or engage with the police. . . . Through a focused, well-facilitated dialogue, where people not only spoke but really listened, not only the process of confederated direct democracy but also the substantive content of it shone as bright as the moon. In the end, hundreds of people who started off trusting the police and a police liaison near unanimously voted (with only five against) to disband the police working group. . . .

I plopped down on the cool concrete under a perfect night sky, with anarchist friends and new friends of all types and political perspectives circled all around in groups, chatting away happily, and I marveled that the hard, frustrating, exhausting, dispiriting work of crafting self-governance and self-organization in a mere five days had, almost unbelievably, forged something beyond and maybe bigger than any of our dreams.

On the evening of day sixteen, that dreamy quality felt almost complete when a whole crew of us decided to crash a party we weren't invited to—being held inside the government building in the middle of our commons:

A bunch of well-heeled, smug, condescending elites were gathering inside city hall to show a fancy PowerPoint presentation about a $50 million renovation of the very plaza that we're occupying—a symbolic slap in the face to most Philly residents. . . . They were talking about how they were dramatically enhancing the city center with a hefty price tag of a privatized-public-space project, with things like a café and free movies. Right where their café is supposed to go now sits our food tents, providing three meals a day and snacks for free to hundreds of people, including many without homes. We air free movies, and sometimes two at a time, many nights. One after one, Occupy Philly residents spoke with eloquence—frequently, I suspect, a newfound eloquence, from the practice we're getting in our general assembly—about all the absurdities of this project, especially its many-million-dollar fountain with lights and smoke—the smoke and mirror of capital gone mad.

We then trooped outside, past security guards and police and barriers, walking back around to our side of city hall plaza, to join our fellow assortment of Occupy Philly folks for our evening's general assembly, already in progress, and this night, it felt like an exuberant celebration of our self-empowerment, our bringing this space, this place, and ourselves to life. . . . There's no better way of us demanding the impossible than doing what seemed impossible a little over two weeks ago.

I knew then that come what may—whether state repression or our own messy-beautiful internal dynamics—we had already won. I knew that "this do-it-ourselves encampment roughly stitched together like some crazy quilt of humanity with things like cardboard, tarps, pallets, duct tape, and string" supplied all of us with an "intense aliveness." Out of nothing, with little to no gestation, we birthed what none of us saw coming, "in all its rich potential: our doing is our demand, our demand is in our doing."

I've been fortunate to have experienced—to have been actively a part of—many "as if we were free" moments. Everything becomes possible; people realize that they have everything within themselves to shape their lives together; time stretches out leisurely; isolation, alienation, and separation fall away, and people feel seen and heard in their fullness; there is a sensual, bonding quality to social relations, as if we've long known and trusted each other. Much more than any theory or piece of anarchist literature, then, those ephemeral yet ethereal experiences are what inspired me to want to curate this anthology. As this collection took shape, however—meaning, as I went on an extended, meandering scavenger hunt around the globe via emails, texts, and private messages to find people who both had a deep relationship to a self-governing space and could write about it eloquently—I found myself more and more humbled.

First, I felt humbled by how much grace each and every contributor to this anthology showed during the incubation period from idea to essay. They all patiently collaborated with me on the rigorous editing process, which involved them doing multiple revisions and refining. This was an especially time-consuming process because I hadn't accounted for what it meant for me—a basically monolingual person—to curate an anthology largely made up of people for whom English isn't necessarily their preferred writing language. Yet that seemed essential to achieve what, for me, is one of the strengths of this book: it offer examples spanning vastly diverse contexts—varied histories and geographies, traditions and cultures, genders and ethnicities, and more—so as to demonstrate that direct democracy is only limited by our imagination, not particular identities or social positions. I trust that if anything is "lost in translation," it is my mistake, not that of the writers in this volume. They each, also, did the impossible: beautifully articulated the complex magnificence and messiness of their collectively self-determined space, yet through their own individual lens.

Much more crucially, I was humbled by the fact that while I could curate this anthology, I couldn't contribute my own piece about a modern-day space of ongoing self-governance—the heart of this project. For all the many times I've felt more alive than ever before within a directly democratic opening—all sorts of micro moments, ranging from a handful of neighbors finding our own ability to determine the life of our block together, to how we use face-to-face decision making so powerfully in, for instance, convergence spaces or anarchist summer schools, and even to those inexplicable times of uprising when tens or hundreds of thousands of people temporarily realize their power together on the streets or in squares—none can really compare to the scale, magnitude, and longevity of the places explored in *Deciding for Ourselves*.

The bittersweet tears I often felt on reading various drafts of the pieces in this book were because I long so much to inhabit such otherworldly communities, which are able to not only create such spaces but also hang onto them. Yet I know that I and so many others might never be able to do so, given the violent social systems that conspire to thwart our every effort. And I carry that bittersweetness still, because with each passing day, before this anthology even makes it into print, some of the self-governing spaces described in these pages are increasingly imperiled, increasingly fragile, and perhaps won't make it much longer.

That said, I do know firsthand what it feels like to have power together—power with and for each other—versus being at the mercy of the forces that lord power over us. It is magical. It is like a disappearing act, with us as rebel magicians waving our collective wand: whoosh, gone is the state's hold on us, and whoosh, in its place is us, (re)discovering that we have all we need to care for each other, through highs and lows. That magic can be grand—as in the stories in this collection—or it can touch us in small, fleeting, or humble ways—as dress rehearsals for such times when we can leap boldly onto the stage of our own lives.

May 2012 was one of those dress rehearsals for me. After a depressing winter following the crushing eviction of Occupy Philly, I journeyed northward to attend the annual Montreal Anarchist Bookfair. I didn't realize I'd be stepping out of the bookfair and into streets overflowing with the romance of a prefigurative rebellion. When a friend said, "You're not leaving, are you?" and a new friend added, "I have an extra room. You can borrow it! Don't leave!" I fell in love with the exuberance all around me and threw myself into it for several months. It was not simply the heady potentiality supplied by what would become the longest student strike in North America—organized and kept alive by a confederation of directly democratic college-based assemblies, themselves part of an educational system won over forty years ago during what was dubbed the Quiet Revolution. It was the unadulterated delight that comes from a social movement having the upper hand, with the politicians and police running to catch up, and repeatedly losing. As I wrote at the time in a blog post:

The people are in power now, but a dispersed, joyous, neighborly power, an imaginatively beautiful display of horizontal solidarity. It's a display that affirms that people can reclaim their lives, their cities, in a way I never dreamed possible. . . . There's a lived practice of having each other's backs here, and making it feel safer and safer for everyone to disobey in ways festive and fierce, but self-controlled. And the more that individuated creativity and social solidarity function, voluntarily, together on the streets and in organizing here, the more additional people seem to join in—like it has opened the door to what's possible, because what's possible, astonishingly, is that people can create a social power that is far beyond a slogan, that is at this moment unstoppable. There are too many people disobeying, collectively, for anything to stop it.

Its unstoppable power came from hundreds and hundreds of thousands of people opening up space via direct action—politically and socially, communally and generously, visually and playfully—to reshape the whole civic landscape, moving from a student strike to what many understood as a social strike. To again borrow from one of my blog posts during this period,

> The "simple" way to strike is by collectively not doing what you're supposed to—business as usual—but instead throwing a wrench into the everyday of all that we do—work, school, leisure, street life, urban space, and anything and everything else. Even if the definitions of "social strike" disagree here in Montreal, people seem to concur that it isn't just about disruption, though that's essential, but what you do during that time of disruption to create something different. It could be said that the idea is for people to "strike" in various ways, and while striking, give new meaning to "social" through the doing of it in new ways. People here often call it the "infinite" or "unlimited" social strike, with the added play on the French word for "strike" (*grève*) as holding within it also the word "dream" (*rêve*).[11] That in itself captures the distinct beauty of a social strike over a general one: that there's a dream inside the making and doing of it.

---

11. Although the student-social strike had large anglophone as well as francophone contingents, French is the official language in Quebec as a result of the settler colonial history here and was dominant in the student-social strike.

Poet Mahmoud Darwish once observed, "Dreamers don't abandon their dreams, they flare and continue the life they have in the dream . . . tell me how you lived your dream in a certain place and I'll tell you who you are."[12] The student-social strike, I commented in another blog post, was "a great big wink between us all," as we reclaimed in "all the little interactions that mean nothing and yet everything, happening in multiple microscopic ways, night after night" during the illegal demonstrations/walks—kicked off when the government passed a special law making demonstrations (*manifestations* in French) a criminal act—that meandered for miles throughout Montreal, or in "student assembly after popular assembly, . . . a notion of what's special among and about us." It hinted at "what's essential for a new society: new social relations."

Over six months, the strike also gestured at social freedom as a sensuous experience. Time itself felt "luxuriously ours," for instance, as if on constant "revolutionary dates" of our own scheduling, "foreshadowing what it would feel like to have all time clocks, alarm clocks, or the constant smartphone clocks banished as our measures of us as 'productive' members of society." Artists ranging from screen printers, filmmakers, and poets to knitters, musicians, and dancers put down their schoolbooks or jobs, formed collectives, and transformed Montreal into a celebration of do-it-ourselves culture, created from passion, not from compulsion or for profit.

In turn, the city itself was "painted" red, thanks to the symbol of this movement: a tiny red square, cut from felt fabric and attached with a safety pin to people's clothes. At first the red square signaled a demand for free education for all, and a way to mark whether one was for or against the student-social strike. Yet it grew into an aesthetic expression of what a tem-

---

12. Mahmoud Darwish, "Now, As You Awaken," in *Now, As You Awaken*, trans. Omnia Amin and Rick London (San Francisco: Sardines Press, 2007).

porarily free society looked and felt like. The rebel-red color was literally everywhere you turned: red chalk, red bikes, red illuminations, red fashion, red sculptures, red ink, red flags, and on and on; Montreal even ran out of red felt at one point. People embraced the color as eye candy for the substantive sweetness of this moment. To offer just one illustration:

I walked into the lush green of the park, and found several hundred people wearing red squares lounging in chatty small groups on the grass, a bandstand covered in red-fabric squares and red-highlighted signs, several big red banners strung between trees plus various red artwork, kids running around with little red squares painted on their faces, bunches of red balloons hanging everywhere, and red-and-white-checked clothes covering picnic tables filled with by-donation food as well as free red literature and a bag full of free red-felt squares. Everyone then gladly formed into a huge three-quarters circle to share strategies decided on by the popular autonomous assemblies of various Montreal neighborhoods.

Equally magical as the color red was the use of sound. For example, someone started circulating the idea of people bringing pots and pans into the streets to bang on with spoons during the nightly illegal manifestations, based on the *carcerolazos* of the 1970s against Augusto Pinochet's military dictatorship in Chile. *Les casseroles* quickly caught on, with tens of thousands of people, including all ages, making "music" with cookware late into the evening. The sound would rise and fall in unison, sometimes clanging and at other times melodic. A dented pot, alongside one's red square, became a symbol of pride.

The casseroles start at 8:00 p.m., but there's no telling when they will stop or where they will go. … It must look amazing from a bird's-eye view, a time-defying swirl of people and noise going every which way, looping around, running into each other, breaking apart into smaller groups, diverging and converging. A red sea of red squares and silvery metal objects. And smiles. So many miles of smiles. . . . It's so festive to stroll down tree-lined streets as the sun sets and stars begin to appear, and people in their homes pop their heads out doors and windows to watch, listen, or wave, or step onto their balconies with their own instruments or cookware to join in.

The most beautiful moment of the casserole nights is when one casserole crew turns a corner and sees another crew—perhaps a thousand in one group, and maybe three thousand in another. For some unexplainable reason, one group will speed up, rushing toward the other, with bigger smiles than ever. And the other group will slow down, oh so slow, until stopping, then a euphoric cheer nearly as loud as the pans will rise up as everyone raises their pots higher still, beating on them loudly. Suddenly, for what's probably only a couple minutes, it's as if the two groups meet in molasses-like slow motion. People look in each other's eyes, really look at each other, turning this moment over in their minds that are trying to comprehend this new time that they are taking and making, in order to maybe make some new world that no one has quite put words to yet.

Beyond the visual and auditory transformation of everyday life, making for wholly new sociability, people embraced the "sensual pleasure [of] direct democracy, like when the sun set this evening over the triangular neighborhood park during our assembly just as we were all marveling at the pleasure of this new form of gathering, discussing, and deciding for ourselves."

We're now in week four of the Popular Assembly of the Mile-End Quarter, which meets every Thursday at a park wedged between two near-highway urban streets. The park is always bustling with dinner picnics and kids running from the "water park" fountains to the playground equipment. Cars, trucks, and motorcycles whiz by. It's hard to hear under the best of circumstances, and like the anticapitalist assembly [I'd recently attended], this neighborhood one necessitates whisper translation. We huddle in a corner of the assembly circle, hardly able to hear the already-circumscribed version of the conversation (the "translators" are always whoever kindly volunteers and are always doing their best!). Most of us English-as-first-language folks don't speak up [out of respect for the French-as-first-language folks and the politics around which language is preferred]. . . .

[Yet a week later], only two people were exclusively French-language listeners/speakers. So it made sense to now whisper translate from English into French for them—a first at our popular assembly. One of the two francophone listeners/speakers looked like she was struggling to hear/understand through the whole of this whisper translation. As we wrapped up the assembly in the gathering darkness, the francophone woman explained, in French, that it was awful having to miss so much of the conversation and yet she truly now understands what it's like to be in our shoes when we're getting French-to-English translation. Her face lit up as she exclaimed, "Together, we've finally broken through the wall of silence between us all!" . . .

Listening. That's what direct democracy sounds like. A whole lot of listening to each other, and what we need, desire, and feel good about doing. Maybe that goes a long way to explaining why neither the tactics, strategies, or aspirations [of this student-social strike] go stale. . . . There are now numerous popular assemblies, begun over the past couple months. They share and borrow from each other. They weren't there at the start of this student strike, nor at the start of the illegal night marches. Now, in many corners of the city, they meet weekly or every other week to talk about issues related to and springing out of the student strike, and many include students, parents, and teachers alongside other neighbors.

In the end, though, when the students returned to school after their summer break, they voted in assembly after assembly, in quickly cascading succession, to stop the strike. The reasons were varied, ranging from explanations that the students were tired, to the more likely notion that the government's ploy to hold elections—supposedly to address the social concerns—had worked. But saddest among these rationales was the sentiment offered by some students that such moments can easily be re-created, easily restarted, so it would be fine to take a time-out. They didn't recognize how precious such spaces are, and how extremely difficult they are to conjure again.

Still, a whole new generation felt a joy that it can't shake to this day, and has tried to put what it experienced into other efforts, toward other such moments. As I remarked at the time,

> If we have any hopes of sustaining such magical manifestations of counterpower—toward some society that doesn't replicate domination and oppression but instead tries its best to experiment with other ways of living and being—joy and its rightfully addictive quality have to remain front and center. Joy isn't going to be enough. The underside of the pots and pans of joy is the nagging, perplexing, heartbreaking question, How do we really transform society? How do we move from street counterpower and making our cities ungovernable, to figuring out ways to shape a society of plenty, self-governed by us all, and still filled with joy? The answers seem even more confusing and distant than ever.

This anthology doesn't supply, once and for all, answers. Yet it does encourage us to remember, as author Ursula K. Le Guin observed, that "it is good to have an end to journey towards; but it is the journey that matters, in the end."[13] We may not be able to say "NO" to most of what's hurting us and the planet, and as a corollary, it's also unclear what we can possibly say

---

13. Ursula K. Le Guin, *The Left Hand of Darkness* (1969; New York: Ace Book, 2010), 237.

"YES" to. But we can journey through spaces where people are promising each other dignified lives in the here and now, and where they are engaging in myriad, marvelous, magical experiments in freedom and autonomy in order to bring that promise into being. That's really all we've ever had, through the warmest or iciest of times. "I know what I'm asking is impossible," Baldwin remarked. "But in our time, as in every time, the impossible is the least that one can demand."[14] And often, as you'll see from the stories ahead, that is a whole hell of a lot.

*

Cindy Milstein has long engaged in anarchistic organizing, contemporary social movements, and collective spaces, and is author of *Anarchism and Its Aspirations*, and editor of the anthologies *Taking Sides: Revolutionary Solidarity and the Poverty of Liberalism* and *Rebellious Mourning: The Collective Work of Grief*. Over the past couple years, they have focused on coorganizing the Institute for Advanced Troublemaking as well as doing support for people facing state repression. Cindy is currently working on another edited anthology, *There Is Nothing So Whole as a Broken Heart: Mending the World as Jewish Anarchists*, and is honored, when called on, to do death doula and grief care.

---

14. James Baldwin, *The Fire Next Time* (New York: Vintage Books, 1993), 104.

A
Horizontal
City

LIVING ANARCHISM IN

BARCELONA'S PERIPHERIES

Stefano Portelli

Some forms of self-government are invisible from the outside. Such invisibility can be the result of limited political self-consciousness within a community or a way of protecting a community's members from unwanted external intrusions. Coherent affirmations of political independence should be unnecessary in terms of recognizing when a community is self-governed. Many people are used to self-managing what is crucial for their lives, yet organizers often fail to see that self-governance due to their own stereotypes of what it should look like. Understanding a city, or producing scholarship about neighborhoods and peripheral areas, should be more than anything else a process of recognizing what forms of social organization already exist in the city that do not fit into the paradigm of the state, regardless of whether they're expressed through explicit or implicit forms of organizing resistance, or recalcitrance, toward the ruling authorities. This would help to both build links with communities that express "anarchism" with their social praxis, outside organized political spaces and social movements, and infuse political content into these self-managed communities—even when their members do not perceive or represent them as such.

Paradoxically, these kinds of autonomies frequently become visible only when they shatter. With urban renewal sweeping the world since the 1950s, many spaces that guaranteed autonomy and forms of self-government to low-income populations have already been destroyed. As psychiatrist Mindy Thompson Fullilove showed in her brilliant book *Root Shock*, even if politicians and planners sometimes offered people better housing than in the supposedly "blighted" centers of the US cities hit by urban renewal, displacement always decimated communal ties and shared senses of belong-ing, plunging people into individualism and conflict.[1] This pattern has been followed by thousands of other cities worldwide since urban renewal en-tered the agenda of most governments; it is a successful tool to reinsert self-managed and autonomous urban communities into the state, making them more dependent and easier to control by erasing the communal spaces and shared history that kept people together. Our task today is to confront urban renewal by both defending communities that still resist it and preserving the memory of those that were wiped off the map, against a narrative of de-velopment that presents old working-class neighborhoods as inherently decaying and obsolete.

This was certainly the case for the Bon Pastor neighborhood, an old public housing estate on the northern edge of Barcelona whose demolition was approved in 2001. Barcelona's city council authorized the relocation of the over twenty-five-hundred inhabitants of the so-called *casas baratas* (cheap houses) into new and taller apartment buildings to be erected nearby. The neighborhood had been built by the same city council back in 1929; its horizontal urban form—small, low-rise homes resembling a village on the edge of the city—was originally meant to isolate migrant laborers on Barcelona's outskirts in order to prevent the spread of revolutionary ideas and practices in the central city. Despite the intentions of its planners, how-ever, the concentration of low-income people in the same neighborhood at the beginning of the Spanish Revolution soon turned Bon Pastor into a hot spot of rebellion, making it one of the places from which *milicianos* (militias) assaulted military headquarters and sent young volunteers to the front lines to battle fascism. Communal occupations of lands and factories

---

1. Mindy Thompson Fullilove, *Root Shock: How Tearing Up City Neighborhoods Hurts America, and What We Can Do about It* (New York: New Village Press, 2016).

around Bon Pastor as well as successful rent strikes and protests against evictions were among the firsts carried on in Barcelona. And the parish priest of Bon Pastor was the first religious figure to succumb, the day after General Francisco Franco's *golpe* (coup) of 1936: after shooting at the crowd that reclaimed his weapons, the priest tried to escape by jumping off the church's balcony, but he fell instead, and nobody helped him while he lay dying in the street. Even the police were afraid of the multitude.

After Franco's victory over and occupation of Barcelona, the neighborhood's political potential was wiped out by reprisals and mass exile. Yet the peculiar spatial distribution of private and public spaces in the neighborhood helped to maintain a living memory of anarchism, embedded in the working-class residents' social practices and habits, although almost never made explicit in their words. Thus horizontality remained an inherent character of the neighborhood, reflected, as we will see, in both its physical space and social organization. Until the demolitions, one could still recognize in Bon Pastor's squares and alleys traces of the "antipolice culture" that anarchists created in Barcelona eighty years ago. It was a culture that, according to historian Chris Ealham in his book *Anarchism and the City*, "championed the rights of 'we,' the community, to determine the way in which the streets were to be used; it was a struggle for neighborhood self-reliance, self-governance and freedom from external authority; a defense of a set of popular urban practices revolving around personal face-to-face ties against the bureaucratic agencies of social control and authority (the police and the courts) and impersonal market forces."[2]

It is a striking contradiction, then, that the ultimate attack on Bon Pastor's urban form and shared ways of life was waged by the left-wing admin-

2. Chris Ealham, *Anarchism and the City: Revolution and Counter-Revolution in Barcelona, 1898–1917* (Oakland, CA: AK Press, 2010), 33.

istration of a city considered among the most progressive in Europe, and several decades after the end of Franco's dictatorship. In 2003, when the municipal bulldozers started to clear Bon Pastor on the orders of the local Socialist and former Communist Parties, I joined in the local struggle against the demolitions, mainly organized by older neighbors. At the same time, together with a group of local residents and other organizers, I began collecting stories and documents as well as observing in detail daily life in public spaces in order to counter the official discourse that depicted Bon Pastor as marginal, passive, and decaying. Our group instead reclaimed Bon Pastor's heritage of resistance and everyday anarchism, which we found alive and well in the interactions of residents in the streets and squares, and reconstructed the history of the neighborhood "from below" through the voices of its elder inhabitants. As a part of what historian Juan José Gallardo referred to as "the red-and-black belt" of Barcelona's peripheries, Bon Pastor, before its recent "verticalization," offers a window into the resilience of what was left of Spanish classical anarchism among the poorest sectors of the urban population in the twenty-first century, and how the ruling authorities, however allegedly progressive, behaved aggressively toward a territory that was, in many aspects, still largely self-managed.[3]

*

Squeezed between the river Besòs—Barcelona's northern frontier—and an inhospitable area of warehouses and manufactures, where the only forms of life were heavy machinery and trucks carrying products to the ring highway, until 2007 Bon Pastor was an extension of almost eight-hundred small,

---

3. José Luís Oyón and Juan José Gallardo, eds., *El cinturón rojinegro. Radicalismo cenetista y obrerismo en la periferia de Barcelona 1918–1939* (Barcelona: Ediciones Carena, 2004).

one-story houses, painted in different colors and patterns, around a grid of parallel alleys only interrupted by three small squares. Most Barcelonans knew it only as a place to buy drugs or the typical marginal neighborhood mentioned in the news; they were often puzzled when they discovered the narrow streets and colorful squares, where kids played around the fountains and elders lingered in the shade of the trees.

Intruders were easily spotted, sometimes called out by groups of younger men and women leaning on the cars parked on the streets or in the squares. A clear sense of who belonged and who didn't was the most evident feature of the area; people chatted or played checkers on the doorsteps, or sat in circles of stools or beach chairs on the pavement, sometimes even in the street. They frequently shut up to wait until you passed, or looked puzzled, trying to find out why you were there and who you were visiting. Older women monitored the street from the doorstep or exchanged visits during housework, while bigger families used the street as an extension of their living rooms, with their bicycles or baby strollers tied to the iron bars of the windows.

Interviewing the residents made us understand how those who lived there perceived their space far differently than how outsiders imagined it. They considered Bon Pastor, first of all, a safe and friendly space to live in, and a place where relations between neighbors were close and respectful. In the words of three older women and a younger resident included in our collective book resulting from these conversations, *La ciudad horizontal*, the neighborhood is more than anything else a familiar place.[4] "We all know each other very well, we all know our defects," said Florentina

---

4. Stefano Portelli, *La ciudad horizontal: urbanismo y resistencia en un barrio de casas baratas de Barcelona* (Barcelona: Editorial Bellaterra, 2015). All quotations from residents are borrowed from this book.

Cánovas, born in 1939 in one of the houses. "Can you understand it? I could quarrel with you today, insult you in any way, and then tomorrow I could come to you and say, 'Do you need to go shopping? Let's go together.' It is just like a family." Another woman echoed her words: "It has been five generations in this house. It means much. My grandparents, my parents, and now it's me; my brothers were also born here, and so were my children, and also three of my five grandchildren were born here." As yet another of the women observed, "To me, this is my village. 'Hello, good morning, how do you do?'... One gives water to your plants, the other cleans your garden." And a man in his thirties explained, "Even if this is considered a marginal neighborhood, it is the most beautiful place you could imagine. What we have here is cordiality and good vibes. People are happily painting their houses, do you see it? One white, the other orange."

Many neighbors we interviewed used phrases such as "our street is the best one in the neighborhood" or "we spend more time in the street than in the house." The word *street* has a crucial place in all the residents' interviews. Although elsewhere *street* expresses marginality or vulnerability—as in *street children*—in Bon Pastor, it was always used to refer to the network of residents living around each street. These sentences thus refer to the collective disposition of the neighbors toward each other, to their conviviality and availability for mutual aid and care. *To be in the street*, or on the doorstep (*en la puerta*), in the words of Bon Pastor's residents, meant primarily the habit of sharing with the other neighbors, helping each other in case of need, and collaborating with as well as supporting the community. "This is very beautiful," said one woman. "I work every day, but if I need a gas tank, my neighbor brings it in, and if the doctor arrives, she will be there [to open the house], and when my mother became too old, it was the same thing." Mutual aid practiced by most families was often mentioned as something that distinguished the neighborhood from other parts of the city. As one resident observed, "Working in Barcelona and talking with colleagues, [I noticed that] what they explain and what we explain is very different. This is a neighborhood of workers; we are all humble, all workers, but we have a human interest in each other that many other places would love to have."

What forged friendship and mutual aid among families in Bon Pastor was obviously sharing the same space: the narrow streets and pavements used as living rooms in the open, as extensions of the once-overcrowded houses. Yet an important part was also played by the collective work of rehabilitating the private and public spaces of the neighborhood, never properly maintained by the local authorities. The city council was quick to evict those who did not pay the rent, but slow in responding to the residents' demands when they needed house repairs. Most neighbors learned to fix their homes on their own, using crafts they often learned on their jobs; this work, though, was almost never authorized by the city council.

All the residents were aware that those who enjoyed a good quality of living in their houses had ensured that with their own efforts, although frequently a communal endeavor by many residents for their neighborhood. "I fixed everything in this house," said Rosa, in her sixties. "I had to build a toilet. I had to build everything. I spent almost five million pesetas. And like me, [this is true for] most of the people: if we didn't maintain the houses, they would fall down." This was also true for the streets, as noted by Ramón Fenoy, a community organizer born in 1950: "This street was all dirt, all stones, and so on. Once, on the day of Sant Joan, my father said, 'We are fed up with having the street like this! We will asphalt it. . . . We will buy mortar, and we will do it.' They did it on the day of Sant Joan. Then, three days later, or whenever the Sant Joan feast was over and the kids returned to school, the director [of the school] passed by, and said, 'What a wonderful street. What work you did. I would not imagine it from the neighbors of this street.' And she wrote to the city council saying that this was something that *it* should have done."

The authorities' lack of interest in maintaining the neighborhood and outsiders' surprise in seeing how effectively residents took care of it themselves was often interpreted as classism against the workers. Thus care and support in repairing the houses and streets was also an affirmation of dissent toward the ruling elites and their prejudices. This collective concern for the neighborhood and its infrastructure, as Franco's regime started winding down, took the form of reclaiming equipment, such as traffic lights or medical facilities—struggles in which most residents took part. Bon Pastor's political structure, which the inhabitants perceived as a collective entity opposing a hostile government, survived the end of the dictatorship. In fact, in most of the narratives we collected, Franco's death and the beginning of democracy in 1976 is not even considered a turning point in their lives—no more so than local events such as the great snow of 1964, when all the residents worked together to shovel out their homes from this unexpected meteorologic event, which also underscored just how architecturally different their neighborhood was from the vertical city growing around them.

It wasn't just upkeep that differentiated Bon Pastor, though; the residents took responsibility for conflicts within their neighborhood. The streets and squares of Bon Pastor were perceived as collectively appropriated by its residents—in some way, as "their" space, despite being formally considered "public" spaces. So the presence of the police, in turn, was regarded by most neighbors as insidious, even many years after the end of Franco's dictatorship. This "antipolice" culture was not explicit, but most residents hid some minor infraction, and relied on their neighbors to keep it concealed. Small deeds such as tapping cable without permission, sub-letting a room under the table, or selling goods without a license could lead to eviction, but few would exploit knowledge of their neighbors' transgres-sions. Impermeability to the state wasn't an abstract ideological stance; it was a collective habitus based on social structures inherited by the neighborhood's anarchist past—such as a vibrant street life and mutual help—that still served each family's individual convenience. For this rea-son, autonomy was not expressed *verbally*, nor organized in meetings and assemblies. It was instead a product of repeated actions performed daily by individuals: people would avoid talking to the police about their neighbors, would alert them if something suspicious happened around their houses, would help each other if they needed aid, and would expect the same from others, scorning those who did not respond to these expectations. The residents of Bon Pastor put more emphasis on maintaining this social dynamic, through gossiping and quarreling, than in regularizing their po-sitions toward the ruling authorities. Self-government was not expressed or admitted verbally; rather, it was performed socially and spatially, as a learned habitus that all residents understood and recognized as their own.

The core of this integrative sociability was a physical space, the street, and more exactly the place where the street met the house: the doorstep. "We are always on the doorstep," a phrase we often collected in our inter-views, conveyed the sense that people were ready to spend time together, chatting with the neighbors, checking each other's kids playing in the street, available to help those who needed it. As Bon Pastor's population and diversity kept growing with the arrival in the 1980s of many families from demolished shantytowns nearby, the existence of this interstitial space, where private and public space met, facilitated an ongoing shared sense of belonging. The doorsteps allowed a third level of sociability, not regulated by the rules of the family or laws of the state, but sustained by the shared customs of everyday interactions that cut distances and smoothed frictions among quite-different families. One resident noted, "If you have a problem with somebody, you know you could find them on the doorstep." As a young resident put it in an interview, "It was as if we lived all in the same house, but in different rooms." Expressions such as "a big family" or "a small village" were frequent, referring to both cherished and hated aspects of social life: readiness to help each other and the inevitable intrusiveness of one's neighbors into one's privacy. This structure of connections was rarely romanticized; it was more often described as something inevitable, something everybody was born into and couldn't do without. It was only when it was shattered by urban renewal that some began to recognize it as crucial for their peaceful interactions and maybe even subsistence.

Indeed, conflict played a substantial part in the social fabric—in particular, the ability to manage conflicts within the community.

When I worked as a child monitor during lunch breaks in Bon Pastor's primary school, my boss, who lived elsewhere in Barcelona, introduced me to the neighborhood with the typical prejudices reserved for a marginal population (dangerous kids, violent families, no hopes, no need to prepare workshops or activities, just watch them closely to avoid them killing each other or running away from the school). After a few months I realized that these stigmatized kids had a far greater capacity for living together than in the other schools I had worked in. While educators and teachers elsewhere were busy separating kids from arguing, Bon Pastor's children seemed to possess some shared "decision-making" techniques to deal with quarrels, preventing adults' intrusions. When a conflict arose, the kids would start yelling at one another, typically claiming that they would hit or kill their opponent, and that if the other dared to touch them, they would call a sibling or other relative to protect them or seek revenge. The kids would keep yelling names of people at one another, while the rest of children—who knew most of the people mentioned—would take sides and gather around the disputants, commenting on what was going on. Through this yelling and commenting, actual violence would be averted; it would be defused by a theatrical device of social and communicative strength, enacted by the disputants and their audience. The educators did not need to enter into the scene or make top-down decisions; they could instead wait and see how the kids managed to solve their conflict, using the social resources that the closely knit community provided them.

This technique also worked for the grown-ups. When two neighbors ran into an argument, most residents of the same street would come out of their houses and lean on the doorsteps or occupy the street, thus creating an audience for the fight and even calling others in: *"pelea, pelea!"* (a fight, a fight!). A circle of people would form around the two disputants, who would then know that every word they pronounced or gesture they performed would be commented on by all the bystanders, and quickly disseminated through gossip to the rest of the neighborhood. The witnesses to the *corrillo* (ring) would not necessarily mediate in the quarrel; rather, they would add tension by teasing the disputants or making fun of the whole argument. But their very presence turned the individual conflict into a public act, which the disputants could close theatrically in front of the community, without need of recurring to physical violence, or designating clearly who won or lost. As in a low-rise version of urbanist Jane Jacobs's thesis in her landmark *The Death and Life of American Cities*, many eyes from the doorsteps make for a safe street; space in Bon Pastor was communally controlled by this interconnection of multiple gazes on each street and through the availability of people to "go out" (*salir*) when they felt they had to do it.[5] This is an *anti-Benthamian* device of vigilance that left no space out of control, but without the need of somebody holding a central position.

A collective ritual enforced this sense of belonging and collective care: Sant Joan's eve, the night of June 23. This feast is traditionally celebrated in Catalonia with solstice bonfires lit by children in the middle of each village. In metropolitan Barcelona, the tradition faded throughout the 1990s with the commodification of leisure and later due to pressures from municipal ordinances for "civil behavior." Bon Pastor's residents, however, kept well alive their tradition of setting up "a disco in each street" for Sant Joan, as one resident put it to me. What all neighbors remember of this festive night, and as I witnessed myself in the few Sant Joans I attended before the neighborhood demolitions began, was the efficacy of the feast's original ritual function: to cleanse the community of "bad spirits"—that is, internal conflicts. Regardless of the disputes and misunderstandings that emerged each year among residents on every street, "in Sant Joan we wiped them all out" (*hacíamos borrón y cuenta nueva*) so as to begin the summer season in peace. The bonfires were considered a symbol of the residents' ability to unite and create something together, using the streets for something much more important than moving from one house to another. The neighbors—Spanish speakers, Catalan speakers, gitanos, and immigrants—would set up long tables on each street and all eat together, putting in common what they had; they would drink *cava*, the Catalan champagne, and dance until morning around the bonfires, which children kept feeding with scrap wood and firecrackers.

---

5. Jane Jacobs, *The Death and Life of American Cities* (New York: Random House, 1961).

The bonfires were extinguished in Bon Pastor during the same years as the city council began replacing the horizontal neighborhood with a new urbanization made of blocks of flats. When the same people found themselves relocated into a *vertical* space, with no access to the streets, with no doorsteps to control social life from, the conflicts among families that the neighborhood managed to control, suddenly exploded; the police found the occasion favorable for intruding much more frequently in the once-protected space of the neighborhood, as more and more residents started to call the police on their neighbors—something previously almost unheard of. In fact, when the demolition of the casas baratas was approved in 1999, all social life in the neighborhood began to change.

What the city council put into question were exactly the elements that held everything together: the houses and streets. The project of demolishing the 784 casas baratas was presented as an improvement for a deprived neighborhood by offering the residents the possibility of buying one of the new flats via a mortgage. While banks and construction firms benefited from the urban renewal plan by selling flats and mortgages to an economically marginal population, both the city council and media presented the old houses as obsolete and decaying so as to promote urban renewal. Although the wealthier sector of the neighborhood saw this policy as a chance to increase their property values, this came at the expense of collective resources on which the poorest residents heavily depended. As in Michael Young and Peter Willmott's classic *Family and Kinship in East London*, urban renewal divided the community.[6]

When we interviewed residents in 2004, most of them were clearly

---

6. Michael Young and Peter Willmott, *Family and Kinship in East London* (Abingdon, UK: Routledge, 2011).

aware that whether they agreed or not with the demolition of their neighborhood, the city council would implement it. The power imbalances had become too great. As the democratic and participatory tools in the neighborhood proved unable to counter the demolitions, many residents stuck to a *symbolic* resistance, claiming that in any case, the city council had no legitimacy to demolish the neighborhood. To the "myth of marginality" that supported urban renewal, as Janice Perlman calls it, the residents of Bon Pastor opposed another myth: what I call the "myth of the marquise."[7]

Many neighbors, even those who did not explicitly oppose the large-scale demolition, claimed that the city council was in fact committing an abuse by imposing urban renewal on the community. They maintained that *the houses did not belong to the city council*, despite all the legal documents to the contrary. "These houses belong to us" (*Estas casas son nuestras*), said many. "They were made for us by an old marquise [*una marquesa*], but during Francoism, the city council took possession of them." As Florentina Cánovas observed, "How did the city council, how did the institutions, take control of these properties? We have very little education, we can't [get] access to understand how it happened." And a seventy-six-year-old resident commented, "This was said many years ago, when my mother was still alive, she died when she was ninety-four, they said so, that a marquise, a duchess, left it for the poor. The [houses] should be for us. . . . My mother used to say, 'I will not see it because I am too old, but maybe you will see it. And maybe these houses, this rumor that this marquise or duchess left them for the poor, someday will be fulfilled.' . . . They would be for us, ours. It would be a gift that this woman made to the poor."

---

7. Janice Perlman, *The Myth of Marginality: Urban Poverty and Politics in Rio de Janeiro* (Berkeley: University of California Press, 1980).

The perception that the demolition of the houses was illegitimate was challenged through a "history from below" repeated by hundreds of residents. The myth of the marquise claimed the right to collective property over what was collectively used and maintained; it challenged the right of the state to dispose of the housing complex as a public good and for the public interest by revealing that it had in fact *appropriated* it so as to exploit it for its own "private" ends. While some neighbors explicitly denounced the demolition of the neighborhood as a speculative project, most of them expressed their discomfort implicitly, through, as anthropologist James C. Scott puts it, the "weapons of the poor" of holding an alternative version of history.[8] They often connected the lack of documents that could confirm the houses belonged to the poor with Franco's occupation in 1939, when the military did indeed take many documents, the Republicans destroyed many others before fleeing, and all the buildings belonging to the workers' unions were seized by the military and never returned. Bon Pastor's poorer residents saw a continuity in the violence and plunder of the fascist dictatorship and the so-called democratic city council now justifying its decision to destroy their neighborhood.

The collapse of the horizontal city of Bon Pastor, represented by the physical demolition of its one-story houses, therefore meant much more than a loss for Barcelona's working-class material heritage. It represents how apparently progressive public policies such as urban renewal, by disrupting the physical spaces where members of the working classes create successful forms of cohabitation and mutual aid, fragment their unity as well as shared lifestyle and culture, privatize and individualize commu-

---

8. James C. Scott, *Weapons of the Weak: Everyday Forms of Peasant Resistance* (New Haven, CT: Yale University Press, 1987).

nities, in order to create allegiances to the state and its ruling elites. Social life in Bon Pastor's casas baratas can be read as a form of successful, though implicit, anarchism: a diverse and marginalized community that managed, to a certain extent, to self-govern the built environment it inhabited, and legitimate its right to decide for itself through shared rituals and myths that created a collective sense of belonging.

Examples of self-governed communities of this kind can be found in countless places throughout the planet, though they are frequently hidden under the cloak of stigma and marginalization. As David Graeber put it in his *Fragments of an Anarchist Anthropology*, we are unlikely to know of self-governed places, since those who actually live in them will most often keep them concealed.[9] This can also be true for urban communities and neighborhoods, which even activists for housing end up despising as backward, marginal, or obsolete, failing to recognize the importance of some concealed forms of autonomy and self-governance of urban spaces. In Barcelona, many activists were trapped in a banal and individualist interpretation of materialism, believing that the relocation of residents into new flats would be a material gain for them, an extension of welfare, rather than a forced dispossession of the essential means of living for the working classes, promoted by the state essentially to defend the interest of construction and financial firms to sell their products to more people.

As urban renewal extends to all continents, more and more cities and neighborhoods of the world are caught in the conundrum of having to choose between their own forms of social organization, or those that are imposed on them by capitalism and the state. We have to defend with all

---

9. David Graeber, *Fragments of an Anarchist Anthropology* (Chicago: Prickly Paradigm Press, 2004).

our strength the possibility of resistance, even when it is expressed in ways other than our own. Perhaps more important, difficult as it might be to read from the outside, and difficult as it might be for those who live it daily to articulate it to us, the struggle against displacement needs to be understood as a fight to sustain "self-governance" among neighbors. In late 2019, as Barcelona rose up against the Spanish state, many residents of Bon Pastor joined the outraged crowds that filled the streets to contest police abuse and institutional violence. They cared little for the independence of Catalonia; they are descendants of Spanish migrants, and often don't even speak the Catalan language. The Bon Pastor residents took part in the marches to reclaim, implicitly, the independence and autonomy of the community they lost under the attacks of state-led gentrification and displacement.

*

Stefano Portelli is an anthropologist at the University of Leicester, currently affiliated with Harvard's Department of Anthropology. He has worked in the peripheral neighborhoods of Managua, Barcelona, and Rome. After years of activist research in Bon Pastor, he began formal training in the anthropology of urban displacement, comparing the effects of forced removal in several cities of the Mediterranean, including Casablanca. Stefano sees anthropology as a tool to challenge the common sense that supports the state.

Pan-Africanism, Social Ecology, and Intimate Direct Democracy

Modibo Kadalie in conversation with Andrew Zonneveld

Modibo is a lifelong revolutionary organizer and academic. He was born and raised in Riceboro, a rural Geechee community of coastal Georgia. In the 1960s, he fled Georgia and moved to Halifax, Nova Scotia, to avoid being drafted into the Vietnam War. During the early and mid-1970s, Modibo was an active member of several radical organizations, including the League of Revolutionary Workers (LRBW), People's Action Committee (PAC), and African Liberation Support Committee (ALSC).

He and I met in 2011, and have worked closely together on a number of projects since that time. Here we have transcribed a conversation where Modibo reflects on his nearly six decades in radical social movements. His writing, organizing, and experience speak to an often-overlooked thread of directly democratic politics within the black civil rights, black power, and pan-Africanist movements. Modibo pulls on that thread to reveal not only the promise of social liberation but also the hope for an ecologically secure future.[1]

*

ANDREW ZONNEVELD: *I'd like to start with big-picture questions. What does direct democracy mean to you? Can you explain direct democracy as a social and political vision? And how did these politics emerge for you?*

---

1. For the full version of this interview, see Modibo Kadalie, *Pan-African Social Ecology: Speeches, Conversations, and Essays* (Atlanta: On Our Own Authority!, 2019).

MODIBO KADALIE: For me, direct democracy is an evolving social vision. My ideas, just like anyone else's, are always developing. In the 1960s and early 1970s, I saw myself as someone who understood race and class, and the dynamics of each, and I was toying with the question of labor and its role in society. The most perplexing question for me, however, was the role of the state. My only political vision at that point in my life was that of a socialist nation-state ruled by the working class, which is what most Marxists desired at that time. This state socialism was supposed to represent the next stage of human social and economic development. Of course, this nation-state was supposed to be large and highly centralized, like the kind we saw in the USSR or China then. And part of that vision was a conception of nationalism that coincided with the emergence of the postcolonial, third world states.

Obviously I no longer hold many of the views that I held then because eventually I began to see that these big, massive, bulky nation-states were contributing to the problem of social oppression, and the emerging postcolonial nation-states of Africa, the Caribbean, and elsewhere in the third world were not solving any problems for their own people. So I started to look at more localized and directly democratic conceptions of socialism, and more intimate forms of democracy, where people could look at themselves and each other, face-to-face, and solve their problems collectively. That's direct democracy to me. I began to see how that tradition was long established in many places around the world, but it was not being recorded.

Direct democracy is also meaningless, though, without a clear understanding of social ecology. We must take to heart all the implications of the assertion articulated by [social anarchist and theorist] Murray Bookchin that, to paraphrase, "there is a social crisis at the basis of every ecological crisis" or "every ecological crisis is in reality a social crisis." Consequently, ecological crises expose social crises. It follows that societies that are organized hierarchically and based on for-profit markets cannot solve or even adequately address any ecological crisis. What is more intimate and integral to our lives and future, after all, than the directly democratic control over our immediate environment and living space? That's the air we breathe, the water we drink, and the food we eat!

We must learn to democratically control the spaces that we inhabit, to expand and take responsibility for them. We can no longer afford to allow others to do this for us. We must learn to do this for ourselves in concert with our neighbors and other communities, which can happen through directly democratic town hall meetings, assemblies, and other popular forums that are empowered to make decisions.

ANDREW: *Would you say this was a gradual or dramatic shift in thinking for you?*

MODIBO: It was dramatic because I also started to see that the people who were articulating the postcolonial vision really did not understand the future of the world. Their ideals were driven more by political expediency than by real critical analysis of the situation. I began to see that the politics they were articulating was also self-perpetuating, since everyone was a part of various Marxist parties and other organizations, none of which seemed to be contributing much insight to the new problems and contradictions that were emerging.

There were two important questions that were not dealt with by these institutions. First was the question of gender and women's liberation. Second was the ecological question, which was largely ignored by many people in these movements. There were struggles against nuclear proliferation at the time, however; for me, that's where I saw the modern ecological movement begin. But ecology did not come into play in most people's analysis of capitalism, racism, or colonialism back then. There were no debates or conversations about it at the time, as far as I could see.

ANDREW: *So would you say that your emerging interest in women's liberation and the ecology movement, combined with a critique of emerging postcolonial nation-states, led you toward a more decentralized vision of socialism?*

MODIBO: Yes, that's where I began to see the relationship between direct democracy and social ecology. I saw direct democracy as the way toward a decentralized, localized, federated type of socialism, and came to the conclusion that in order to understand democracy in its fullest dimension, we also have to understand social ecology. When Bookchin advanced the idea that human society was a part of the natural world, since it was created by human beings as they evolved, that was helpful for me. That is to say, the question of how humans relate to the rest of the natural world must be incorporated into how we understand the future of labor, race, sex, and class. So my vision of direct democracy and social ecology evolved in a symbiotic relationship with one another. A directly democratic vision of social progress involves a social ecology and direct democracy where people are engaged in a process of healing with the earth, as both have been scarred by capitalism. Of course, there was certainly ecological destruction prior to capitalism, but there's really nothing like capitalism when it comes to ecological degradation and catastrophe. The scale is so massive that it's almost hard to comprehend.

ANDREW: *A lot of people hear the word "democracy" and conflate this term with a form of representative, hierarchical government that's currently mod-*

eled by various nation-states across much of the world. In the United States, we are taught in school that democracy is essentially synonymous with the republic and is almost exclusively defined as participating in elections. I think for many people, this is an important intellectual barrier to overcome. To that end, can you talk for a moment about the difference between so-called representative democracy and direct democracy?

MODIBO: Representative democracy is really not democracy at all. It's a kind of sham. Essentially, it's a form of government in which a ruling nation-state asks a group of people called "citizens" (who by the way are not really citizens but instead more like consumers) to simply vote for elite representatives who will then create the policies that govern everybody's lives. To me, that is inherently undemocratic. In this system, people are bound by decisions that a ruling minority has made on their behalf, rather than by decisions that they make together among themselves.

This so-called representative democracy is the same thing as the republic, which historians have venerated as the supreme form of democratic social organization. It's not. Republican forms of government, with their parliaments, congresses, executive branches, judicial branches, and all these things, are simply bureaucratic expressions of the lack of democracy in society.

In a direct democracy, there is no institution of representation. The democracy happens between the actual "citizens" themselves, who are making face-to-face decisions about their society. That precludes professional policy makers, and in doing so, gets rid of corruption, which is usually born from people seeking patronage from one political party or another. Absent these forces, you can engage in a face-to-face interaction wherein everybody has a common need to live a more fully developed life. You can only

achieve that for everybody by sitting down, or gathering together in assemblies, and talking about their issues, circumstances, and relationship to
the natural world—not just talking shit about each other! [*laughs*].

ANDREW: *So if the word "democracy" is derived from the Greek, meaning*
"the people rule" (and of course, I don't mean to venerate ancient Greek so-
ciety at all), then is the key to emphasize egalitarian self-governance among
everyday people?

MODIBO: Yes, self-governance among everyday people who are not driven
by consumerism or the private ownership of property. And people do it all
the time. When there is some kind of emergency or immediate threat to a
collective group of people, they organize themselves and counter the threat
as best they can. They shore up the dam. They try to put the fire out. They
provide housing for refugees. They find a way to feed everybody if there is
food available.

   When I was involved in movements in Detroit in the 1960s and 1970s,
I saw people on picket lines, I saw people striking, I saw students sitting in
and occupying buildings; they would sleep on the floor and share food.
People were collectively organized, and they were *self*-organized. Nobody
had to tell them to clean the bathrooms; they just did it. They kept their
space clean. When they got up in the morning, they folded up their mat-
tresses. They called press conferences. They had freedom schools and
teach-ins. All these are, to me, democratic forms of organizing.

ANDREW: *I know that when you were in Detroit, you became involved with*
the LRBW and participated in a lot of organizing in communities there.
Eventually you had a political break with the LRBW, stemming from your
desire for the group to abandon the rigid structure of a Marxist-Leninist

vanguard party. So from what you're mentioning here, would you say that witnessing a more horizontal, collective organizational principle in practice in the various movements that sprang up while you were in Detroit influenced your push for more democracy within the LRBW?

MODIBO: Yes, it did. Sometimes those picket lines would be all night long, all day long, and sometimes the sit-ins would be too. We had a successful strike for the establishment of black studies at Highland Park College. The strike lasted a whole month. People fed one another. They looked out for one another's needs. When there was some minimal amount of conflict, it was easily settled because everybody was aligned in the purpose for which they were there, you know what I mean? We established a real community. It's an amazing thing to behold. But to a person who is not looking, they won't see it.

ANDREW: *Can you tell me more about the push for direct democracy within the LRBW? What inspired you toward this direction? You were influenced by the writings of pan-African socialist C. L. R. James during this time, right?*

MODIBO: Willie Gorman, who worked at the Facing Reality bookstore on Woodward Avenue in Detroit, introduced me to James's writing. He gave me a copy of *Notes on Dialectics*, which was the first thing I read by James. A little while later, I read *History of Pan-African Revolt*. But he slipped a copy of *Every Cook Can Govern* into that stack of pamphlets and … I honestly didn't find it interesting at the time [*laughs*]. Later, of course, I did.

The LRBW was part of a large wave of democratization that was sweeping the entire world then. The fundamental role of the LRBW was to democratize the trade union movement. In other words, to get rid of racial discrimination in the trade union movement. Yet because the movement for black studies and the democratization of the universities had already traveled a long way down the road, these young student organizers got ahold of the LRBW and started projecting it as a black Bolshevik party.

After the LRBW was formed, it began to incorporate all manner of local community organizations under an "executive board." We assumed that the organizers on the ground would have some autonomy, and would have their opinions heard and could vote on certain decisions. We had a limited, bourgeois democratic structure, or at least we thought there was some democracy in the organization, but it was not to be—not at all.

By 1971, the LRBW had formed a central committee. The executive board was on top of that, made up of the principle founders of the LRBW. This body was supposed to be elected out of the central staff, which was supposed to be made up of the heads of all the component organizations. I was on the central staff as a representative of the PAC and Highland Park.

The LRBW was bureaucratic. It was organized so that the people at the top were doing the thinking, and the people in the middle and at the bottom were doing the work. The experience and knowledge of the rank and file never reached the top of the organization in any meaningful way. So the organization was fettered from the beginning.

I got purged from the LRBW, along with five other organizers on the central staff, including my wife at the time, because we pushed for some kind of flatter organizational structure or more democracy within the organization.

We didn't really have a well-defined idea of direct democracy at that point, but we were critical of the fact that the LRBW never really advocated taking over the factories or seizing the means of production as a source of power. It was really modeled as a vanguard party, outside the production process. It was talking about taking political power as a Marxist-Leninist party, not as workers taking direct control of their lives. That's why people like Kimathi Mohammed and James found themselves in conflict with the LRBW.

The LRBW was many different things to many different people, and could never really find its focus or grounding because of its structure, which was fundamentally antidemocratic and authoritarian. Black people got into the unions and had caucuses in the unions, but the LRBW's structure wouldn't allow the organization to do much beyond that. But it did succeed in introducing a radical strain into the larger labor movement.

Back then, people who called themselves black nationalists would run the gamut of beliefs about how black activists should organize in North America. There were those who thought that black people represented (or should represent) an actual separate nation, and desired some form of black statehood, and others who simply wanted independent and autonomous black revolutionary organization.

I was not a nationalist, but I was of the belief that black people should organize independently. I got that from James's *Negro Question in America*, which he had written in 1948. Further, C. L. R. had an impact on black nationalism through his *History of Pan-African Revolt*, which had recently been reprinted at this time, so a lot of people were reading that and it was popular.

C. L. R., however, really wanted local organizers in Detroit to circulate his *Every Cook Can Govern* pamphlet, but it wasn't black enough for most of us. It was about the Greek city-states, and the way in which they organized themselves directly and governed themselves. But the problem with this pamphlet, as far as we were concerned, was that the Greeks had slaves, they didn't include women in their democracy, and foreigners were not included. So we looked at that structure as kind of elitist.

C. L. R. was able to overcome this basic criticism, explaining that what we needed to do was pick out the directly democratic themes or elements in the history, and see how they might be applied. So that's how C. L. R. influenced me and Kimathi in this direction. At the time, there was a group of us looking for a new way forward because this vanguard party thing was not getting us anywhere, you know? We saw it as elitist.

Anyway, a group of us had been purged from the LRBW in April 1971, and on June 12 and 13 of that year, we hosted two lectures by C. L. R. at the YMCA on Woodward Avenue in Detroit. The first lecture was about the meaning of the dialectic. The second lecture was supposed to be about the idea of the vanguard party, but C. L. R. really didn't touch on that question at all. At the beginning of the lecture, he posed a few questions to the audience, but the room fell deathly silent. The executive committee of the LRBW was there, those who'd been purged were there, and some people from Lansing, Michigan, were there too. So the room was charged, but nobody wanted to engage.

Some of us thought C. L. R. would take the position that the vanguard party couldn't get us anywhere, but he never did. We were trying to get the question of the party settled so that people would understand that the party is not black power; it's black elitism.

In 1972, there was the Gary Convention, which was a consolidation of black mayors and other elected officials in the Democratic Party. That same year was the beginning of the ALSC in Greensboro, North Carolina. In addition, there was the beginning of the Caribbean Unity Conference, from which the Sixth Pan-African Congress (6PAC) emerged. So 1972 was an important year, and those of us in the PAC and Garvey Institute had developed a clear critique of the vanguard party, and we wanted to publish something about it. Of course, there were a lot of different groups calling themselves the vanguard party at that time. They were all reading the same book—Vladimir Lenin's *What Is to Be Done?*—and were misapplying it, in our view. In summer 1973, we held a conference in Detroit to discuss this problem. We called it the First Organization and Spontaneity Conference. At that event, Kimathi made an impressive speech, so we all decided that we would support him in publishing his pamphlet *Organization and Spontaneity: The Theory of the Vanguard Party and Its Application to the Black Movement in the U.S. Today* in the hope that we could put this question of the vanguard party to rest. After he wrote it, we all helped circulate it. That historical moment, the publishing of that pamphlet, represents the conjuncture of the LRBW, ALSC, and 6PAC.

ANDREW: *Can you tell me more about the results of these efforts you made surrounding the LRBW? What did you glean from all this? Can you tell me how this experience affected the ideas as well as organizing of you and your comrades?*

MODIBO: You have to have a keen eye to see how mass movements are unfolding in front of you. So I started to watch people and how they organize themselves. Like I've said before, in all these catastrophes that are happening now as a result of climate change, you can see people helping one another. Some of them are racist; that might be true. Some of them are homophobic; that also might be true. But when it comes down to the bottom line, they are human beings and help one another. You know, I believe what [anarchist and geographer] Peter Kropotkin said: there is an instinct for mutual aid and support among people.

ANDREW: *I'm glad that you're bringing this up. Tens of thousands of people have been displaced and killed by ecological catastrophes all over the planet in the past few years. I think community self-organization in the face of such hardship and loss is going to be something that will be discussed more frequently as time moves forward.*

What you said reminds me of something that Kōtoku Shūsui, the famous Japanese anarchist, wrote while he was visiting the United States in 1906. He was living in Oakland, California, for a few months and witnessed the Great San Francisco Earthquake. The destruction was horrifying, especially the fires that devastated the city following the earthquake itself. But while all this was happening, he saw people helping one another—people who didn't even like or know each other well. They came together and even provided food for one another.

Kōtoku later said that in the days following the earthquake, everyone in the San Francisco Bay Area was living in a state of anarchist communism.[2] This became formative for him in his emerging anarchist politics. According to Kōtoku, the fire was not to blame for the hunger, death, and cold suffered by the people after the earthquake. In fact, it was the social order that was to blame for not supplying people with the security they needed in the first place. Following the disaster, people seemed to instinctively know that something distinct was needed if they were going to survive, so they organized with their neighbors to provide aid to all who were in need. When Kōtoku returned to Japan from California, he declared himself a committed anarchist, and from that time onward, his speeches and writings emphasized the extraordinary collective ability of people to organize themselves.

2. F. G. Notehelfer, *Kōtoku Shūsui: Portrait of a Japanese Radical* (London: Cambridge University Press, 1971), 129–31.

MODIBO: It's true! People don't have to vote on that kind of stuff, you know? They just see what needs to be done and do it. They organize it themselves. Someone brings a shovel, someone else brings a bag, one guy lifts this, one guy carries that, someone else drives the pickup truck—you can see it in action.

Beginning with my experiences in Detroit, I gradually learned to look at the world from an antihierarchical point of view and started to see everything differently. When I saw people taking blows from the police on the streets in Detroit, these were people who typically might not be involved in activism. But they were out there taking heroic stands, throwing stuff at the police and all that. The spirit for mutual aid is there.

That's what it's all about: decentralizing everything and making sure there is a continuous revolution. Kropotkin had that pretty much down. [Marxist theorist] Leon Trotsky also said that. Trotsky wasn't right about much, but he was right about the need for continuous revolution. But continuous revolution can't exist within the context of a nation-state.

ANDREW: *Absolutely. Let's talk more about your work within the ALSC.*

MODIBO: I mentioned before that the LRBW represented the democratization of the US labor movement. The ALSC is part of that same wave of democratization. It was the internationalization of this sweeping democratic movement that took on two forms: the ALSC and 6PAC, which really started with and were part of the Caribbean Unity Movement, and on the other side of the Atlantic Ocean, the new neocolonial nation-states that were taking form in Africa. A lot of people thought that these new states were the ultimate goal of black power, but those states achieved only the same limited goals such as the running of black candidates for political office in the United States.

The ALSC had two goals: to raise money for anticolonial liberation movements on the African continent, and mobilize people in their local communities to support these struggles. We did not accept big corporate donations. We raised money from the grass roots. We called it "shakin' cans." You know, going into the community and bringing attention to the fact that black people were struggling for their freedom against colonialism in Africa. Of course, the US mainstream media had not even acknowledged those struggles at all.

ANDREW: *That's so important because in the United States, the awareness of African liberation struggles in the 1970s was communicated almost exclusively through grassroots efforts like yours. But I'm curious, where did you go when you would shake the can? What kinds of locations or events in the community did you frequent?*

MODIBO: One thing that we did in Detroit was that we got ourselves an old Bell and Howell movie projector, and we actually went into neighborhood bars, set up the projector and screen, and asked the bartender if we could show the film *A Luta Continua* (*The Struggle Continues*), which was about the fight for independence in Mozambique.

When we showed the film in the bars, people would turn around in their seats and really become engaged, like, "Wow! Where are black people doing that?" This was in 1971 to 1972. Of course, in Detroit we had just experienced a wave of insurrections, so many people were keenly aware that this is the way you do it! [*laughs*].

We raised plenty of money. By the time we had our second national convention, we had raised something like six or seven thousand dollars. We learned to evaluate the effectiveness of our cadre by how many people we could mobilize and how much money we could each raise. Keep in mind that the antiwar struggle had reached a certain level too. The youths and radicals were mobilized. They were used to marching for international causes, be it in Vietnam or, in our case, the African liberation struggles. We also had pamphlets that we passed out with names like [South Africa's Nelson] Mandela and [Zimbabwe's Robert] Mugabe—people whom some folks hadn't even heard of. By the time we became known in the community for doing this work, we could go out on the street corner and shake cans.

The reason we would shake the cans is because we didn't want big money. We wanted people to put nickels, dimes, and quarters in there. The more quarters we had, the more people we had reached. Parents would give kids money to put in our cans. So the ALSC was really a grassroots mobilization effort on this side of the Atlantic to support the anticolonial struggle in southern Africa, on the other side of the ocean.

ANDREW: *That's a remarkable effort. You not only raised funds for the independence fighters but also played an important role in educating folks in the United States about what was going on in Africa at the time.*

MODIBO: Yeah, that's what it was. We also did not allow elected officials to speak at our rallies. The black politicians who presented themselves as the leaders or even embodiment of the black freedom movement were not allowed to take the podium. That was a strict rule that we decided on together.

ANDREW: *That leads me to wonder how your local branches of the ALSC collectively navigated the question of the emerging postcolonial political leadership in Africa and the Caribbean. I know your own individual opinion was quite skeptical, but how did that play out in your organizing?*

MODIBO: We had a clear critique of neocolonial governments, but we hoped that the newest governments that were coming to power at that time would see that neocolonialism was just as bad as colonialism. The anglophone Caribbean, of course, was already taken over by neocolonial governments by this time. We did not support them at all. In fact, there were a lot of working people struggling against the neocolonial governments—and that's who we supported.

During the organizing for the 6PAC, this tension broke wide open. They couldn't even have organizing meetings in the Caribbean because the governments prohibited such meetings. And as you know, eventually the nongovernmental delegations from the Caribbean were not even allowed to be seated at the 6PAC.

ANDREW: *Right, so some of the major heads of state like Tanzanian prime minister Julius Nyerere and Guyana's Forbes Burnham maneuvered to restrict the participation of grassroots delegations from the Caribbean. They wanted only official representatives of postcolonial governments, where such existed, to attend the 6PAC. In response, James and [Guyanese intellectual] Walter Rodney denounced the congress, which took place in 1974. James refused to attend at all. You attended, though, right?*

MODIBO: Yeah. In the United States, we obviously did not have a postcolonial, black-led government, so that restriction really didn't apply to us. And we were mostly successful in keeping black politicians and the Congressional Black Caucus out of our organizing efforts as much as possible.

The 6PAC also received a lot of resistance from black people living in Britain and France. When these folks heard that the congress was being sponsored by the governments in Guinea, Ghana, and Tanzania, a lot of them walked out—especially when they heard [Guinean president] Sékou Touré's name.

You see, at that particular time, there were contentious struggles within these states in Africa. The states were not stable at all, and were subject to all kinds of political coups and factions and everything. But there were certain governments that were regarded as being pan-African oriented, like Nyerere's Tanzania. On the other side of the ocean, when Burnham took power in Guyana, the subsection of pan-Africanists that lacked any real class analysis embraced Burnham, even though he was repressing both Afro-Guyanese and Indo-Guyanese people in Guyana.

ANDREW: *I'm glad you mentioned Guyana because it reminds me of Eusi Kwayana's book* The Bauxite Strike and the Old Politics, *which describes a directly democratic labor strike that was initiated by Afro-Guyanese mine workers in 1971. Burnham was nationalizing the bauxite mines, but when the workers realized that during the transition to nationalization the ruling party had absconded with a large portion of their pension fund, they rebelled. They took over their union hall, and organized directly democratic councils and committees through which they collectively made decisions about their strike efforts. Their slogan was "Every man is his own leader, and we are leaderless."*

As you know, the strike ended with mixed results. Some people got their pensions back, but others weren't so lucky. Kwayana, however, eventually saw these events as an important moment in Guyana's decolonization, when people "tried out new forms of organization," and "showed the capacity of alienated workers for self-assertion, self-determination, for responding to situations, and for creative development of workers' government."[3]

Later on, this strike was followed by the similarly directly democratic Landless Sugar Workers' Rebellion in 1973. During that movement, Afro-

---

3. Eusi Kwayana, *The Bauxite Strike and the Old Politics* (Atlanta: On Our Own Authority!, 2014), 76.

Guyanese and Indo-Guyanese sugarcane tenant farmers worked together to squat and seize land from Bookers, a British sugar company. They formed "people's committees" among themselves in order to keep track of and evenly divide the expropriated land. These squatters hoped that Burnham's government would recognize their actions as part of nationalization and economic revolution, but instead Burnham sent his police to viciously attack the squatters.

I think Guyana is a powerful example of how social and economic revolution is not really compatible with statecraft and hierarchy. Even heads of state who claim to be socialists will undermine working-class self-determination every chance they can get because their authority depends on holding a certain degree of control over people's lives while also reproducing many of the exploitative relationships that existed under previous regimes.

MODIBO: That's true, and through involvement in the 6PAC, I began to see with my own eyes that this class thing was real. I learned what class conflict looked like in the postcolonial/neocolonial moment.

While the history of these movements in Guyana is inspiring, it's also important to remember that the mere presence of popular assemblies in a movement or community does not necessarily indicate the presence of direct democracy. Sometimes these assemblies are still quite removed from the type of intimate contact that people need to develop some kind of real understanding about who they are—that humans are part of nature, and human society is a natural development. Intimate social connections are required to see humanity as anything other than removed from nature.

Unfortunately, popular assemblies can often become spaces where people talk, listen, and inform one another, but where frequently nothing is decided. The movement in Jackson, Mississippi, is one example of this. In 2017, Cooperation Jackson ran a municipalist campaign to elect Mayor Chokwe Antar Lumumba and advance a kind of directly democratic politics. Even before the campaign, it had organized popular assemblies in Jackson because the people there wanted control over their community, but in the end, Cooperation Jackson fell into the trap of so-called participatory democracy. People in Jackson come together to discuss and propose ideas in the assemblies, but ultimately Mayor Lumumba makes all the decisions. That's just another form of representative democracy. The people are not yet making the decisions themselves. Their role is only advisory, and the basic hierarchy of state power is still in place, now legitimized by the rhetoric of direct democracy.

When communities can get together and actually decide things for themselves, however, that's something else. I sincerely hope that the movement in Jackson will get there. But to do it, you need to take away some people's property. I don't mean nationalize, but you need to take collective control over the way in which your society sustains itself locally. I think many people in Jackson understand the need for communal property. It cuts down on corruption too, because without private property, people don't have much vested interest in advancing themselves individually.

By the way, corruption is just a form of political patronage, that's all. If one group of people gets something from its elected officials, that's considered corruption by another group of people [*laughs*]. But that's how it works. Hierarchical government is always inherently corrupt. For example, a lot of black people want more patronage from the Democratic Party. They want a "piece of the pie" and a seat at the table where the pie is divided. What an atrocious analogy! You're talking about dividing a pie when you should be worried about how the pie is baked in the first place! We don't just need an even slice of pie for everyone but also an even share of responsibility in creating the pie.

It's important to clarify that participatory democracy is not direct democracy at all. Most of all because it lacks the necessary intimacy. And too often it only means participating in a conversation while someone else ultimately decides what to do.

Yet there are always movements, societies, and communities in existence that are intimate and locally organized, where no one person owns every damn thing, and people can talk to each other and work things out among themselves; where everybody is relatively equal. Our most immediate work should be to learn how to adjust our vision so that we can see these examples for what they are.

ANDREW: *Pan-Africanism is often assumed to be a set of politics that is mostly concerned with establishing and defending the authority of postcolonial state power in Africa, the Caribbean, and elsewhere. In contrast, your personal understanding of pan-Africanism clearly rejects the nation-state outright and instead is rooted in a directly democratic social current that runs through the long history of anticolonial movements. Can you briefly explain why you think it is important for pan-Africanism to break with the idea of the nation-state? And what does this mean for the future of the pan-African movement?*

MODIBO: One thing I owe to C. L. R. is that he never called himself a black nationalist. He advocated independent black organization, but that's not the same thing as nationalism.

The concepts of the nation-state and pan-Africanism have been related to each other, in one way or another, throughout the history of anticolonial struggles. The nation-state and representative government, including all forms of indirect democracy or republicanism, are all in the way of direct democracy, social ecology, and the realization of human social freedom. By now, these models of governance have all been revealed as bankrupt and belonging to the old oppressive politics of an earlier time, even though they linger, casting a long shadow and foul stench in the present period.

The problem of human survival in the face of rapid and catastrophic climate change is beyond the understanding of these antiquated politics, which cannot grasp the scope of this catastrophe that by its very nature demands a new politics beyond the realm of exploitative global capitalist enterprise, zealously protected by the armed forces of competing empires.

Since we know there is a social crisis at the basis of every ecological crisis, or that every ecological crisis is in reality a social crisis—again, I'm grateful to Bookchin for this framework—consequently ecological crises can expose social crises. And in the twenty-first century, we can now confidently say that hierarchically organized societies cannot solve or even adequately address ecological crises. In fact, such societies—with their nation-states, empires, and capitalist markets—have shown themselves to be the cause of widespread ecological destruction.

If, as recent history demonstrates, pan-Africanism is going to be defined by the unity or clustering of black-ruled nation-states and black capitalism, it serves no purpose other than the continued oppression of black exploited classes under black elites. Such models are as inadequate to black liberation as they are to solving climate change.

The concept of pan-Africanism, however, is perfectly compatible with the development of locally decentralized and directly democratic institutions in areas where African people live and work. In other words, we need a pan-African social ecology.

The vague outline of a peoples' pan-Africanism began to emerge within the discussions and clashes of concepts and ideas that were playing out within the 6PAC in Dar es Salaam, Tanzania, in 1974. It was by no means the dominant perspective at the congress. Yet since that time, it has become clear that when most organizers try to conceptualize pan-Africanism, they typically mean it in the sense of a pure Nkrumahist statecraft. Some people, inspired by Kwame Nkrumah, even talk of a simplistic "United States of Africa." Clearly such a conceptualization involves a centralized autocratic apparatus with concentrated state power that governs from the top down, or even a continental republic or centralized Organization of African Unity [founded in 1963 to encourage solidarity between African nations while eliminating colonialism] that includes some diasporic representation, much like a larger version of the Zionist state of Israel. Sometimes more progressive black organizers see this large, centralized, united African state as some kind of "socialist" one-party state, similar to the old USSR, or present-day China or Cuba.

Both of these notions will take us in a backward direction.

To me, pan-Africanism is useful as a directly democratic people's framework, particularly applied to local struggle. It can be applied in the same way as the indigenous people's or working-class people's movement: not for the reform of the nation-state or a nationalist movement, but as a decentralized, local antistate movement where black and/or indigenous people live and struggle; a nonexclusive movement including all local organizers who are engaged in autonomous self-organization and the creation of directly democratic institutions that can respect all oppressed people.

ANDREW: *What might those kinds of politics and movements look like in the world today, and where should we be looking for their emergence?*

MODIBO: I think we need to be paying attention to disaster relief and the kinds of popular self-organizing that it entails. In the twenty-first century, we have all witnessed the complete devastation of many of the Caribbean islands by a recent rash of hurricanes. Most people in the United States are aware of the almost-complete destruction of infrastructure in Puerto Rico and the Virgin Islands, which are of course US territories. We must look at these cases for signs of directly democratic decision making that is happening within the small communities that dot these islands. We must look closely in order to see the path of their recovery.

In another example, however, the complete devastation of the infrastructure of the small island of Barbuda by Hurricane Irma in 2017 has resulted in a serious struggle against the black central government of Antigua and Barbuda. In the wake of the hurricane, the government in Antigua completely evacuated the population of some fifteen hundred island residences in Barbuda. After the storm passed and the island was devastated, the government instituted a plan for land privatization under the guise of recovery, very much against the desires of the Barbudan people. The island of Barbuda is much smaller than the larger tourist-dependent Antigua, and maintains a history of collective landownership and a collective self-sustaining economy that dates back to slavery.

Barbudans to this day have retained their autonomy despite a strong push for them to develop a tourism industry. They remain steadfastly reliant on subsistence agriculture and the production of food for direct consumption on the island, and have also successfully maintained a collectivized fishing and seafood-packing industry. The central government is now seeking to use foreign private investment to construct a super hotel on Barbuda and destroy the last vestiges of autonomous self-governance within that small region of the Caribbean world. The locals, however, have engaged in direct action and clashes with the police in an attempt to stop these modern-day enclosures.

This history of collective landownership by formerly enslaved Africans within the islands of the Caribbean reveals a unique and lesson-laden legacy. Within the islands and areas of land adjacent to the Caribbean Sea, wherever land was available, newly emancipated Africans simply took the land for themselves. After all, they had spent generations laboring on it. And because of residual cultural practices, to the extent that they were not completely destroyed by prolonged enslavement, emancipated Africans typically used this land collectively. You even find this tradition in the Reconstruction era of the southeastern United States immediately following the Civil War. Africans who worked the rice and cotton plantations on the coast of Georgia emancipated themselves when the plantation owners fled. They took control of the land and began the process of redistribution among themselves. This was the origin of the Ogeechee rebellion and marked the start of the proliferation of Geechee communities.

The best-documented movement of this type, though, was Guyana's postemancipation village movement, which was written about by our friend and fellow traveler Kwayana, the great Guyanese sage you mentioned earlier. That movement of collective land redistribution by black folks lasted from the 1820s right down through the period of the anticolonial struggle in the mid-twentieth century.

More contemporarily, we can look to the Ujamaa village movement in 1968 in what had by then become Tanzania. Tanganyika had become independent in 1961 and merged with Zanzibar in 1964 to become Tanzania. The village movement was a popular push for more local autonomy among several rural areas as the rapidly consolidating nation-state under the rule of a single party was being felt at the village level. The Tanzania African National Union, the ruling political party in 1968, began to steer the self-governing initiative within certain rural villages with its own policies and directives, co-opting the struggle in the interest of the state.

As historians, we have to learn to render the statements of state leaders and writings of elitist scholars as secondary effects of the more primary social motion that we seek to understand in its essence. Nyerere's words, however inspiring or poetic they may seem, are meaningless if we fail to grasp the fundamental repressive or co-optative response of the state in opposition to the directly democratic social and ecological action in this context.

It is clear to me that throughout the colonial world and most especially within the anticolonial national liberation struggles themselves, there is evidence of directly democratic movements and social formations—weak and strong. We must uncover them, and develop a new understanding of how capitalism and state power have altered the direction of these postcolonial societies. Much of history has to be rethought and rewritten.

*

Modibo Kadalie is the author of three books, *Internationalism, Pan-Africanism, and the Struggle of Social Classes* (2000), *Pan-African Social Ecology* (2019), and *Intimate Direct Democracy* (2020). In the 1970s, he served as a member of the central staff in the League of Revolutionary Black Workers and was chair of the People's Action Committee in Highland Park, Michigan. He was a founding member of the African Liberation Support Committee and a delegate to the 1974 Sixth Pan-African Congress in Dar es Salaam, Tanzania. Modibo recently retired from a long teaching career in higher education, having taught in historically black colleges and universities across the United States and in South Africa. In 2017, he founded the Autonomous Research Institute for Direct Democracy and Social Ecology in Midway, Georgia. Andrew Zonneveld is a historian, parent, and activist from Atlanta, Georgia. He is the founder and managing editor of On Our Own Authority!, an independent radical publishing house, and has been an organizer of the Atlanta Radical Book Fair since 2016.

From
#RickyRenuncia
Protests
to People's
Assemblies in
Puerto Rico

Jacqueline Villarrubia-Mendoza and Roberto Vélez-Vélez

A microphone sat in the center of a crowd under some trees in Plaza Las Delicias in Ponce, the largest city on the southern coast of Puerto Rico. Some of the people present occupied the concrete benches on the outer perimeter of the circle around the microphone. Others had brought beach chairs or sat on the ground, and some stood along the edges, arms crossed, looking in. It was a little past six in the evening.

Veronica, a young woman from the University of Puerto Rico at Ponce, called the assembly to order and welcomed the crowd of some eighty people, noting that many had crossed paths during recent protests. "In the many conversations that emerged while the people of Puerto Rico took to the streets to request the resignation of Governor Ricardo Rosselló, we shared the same question: 'What will happen after Ricky resigns?'" she said. "So we met a few days ago to organize the proposal that we bring to you today: the people's democratic assembly." This was the first of many people's assemblies, called by diverse groups across the island to discuss the next stage in Puerto Rico's newly acquired experience in popular democracy.

The exercises in direct democracy that sprouted during the massive protests—taking the form of everything from marches that shut down the streets, to dance, horseback riding, and motorcycle demonstrations, among others—led to the resignation of Rosselló on July 25, 2019, and crystallized for Puerto Ricans a consummation of popular power. The outcome confirmed that an organized group of people can exert enough pressure to force a détente on the state. Following Rosselló's resignation, however, many have expressed concerns about possible demobilization. Some fear that as people return to the routines of life, the fiery resistance struggles of July will gradually fade from our collective memory. Were the protests and marches the beginning and end of this political awakening? How far can this newly acquired power be taken?

Puerto Ricans now explore the breadth of these challenges with the formation of people's assemblies. Assemblies began in August on different parts of the island, from Ponce, Mayagüez, Lares, and Utuado to Caguas, Gurabo, San Juan, and Carolina, as word spread with the help of hashtags such as #asambleadepueblo on social media. Two months after being established, there were approximately thirty-one across the island. Different sectors of civil society have convened these assemblies with the mission of deliberating on how to provide continuity to the mobilized populace and entering into deep conversations about governance.

These newly emerging spaces initially took different shapes, but all through an organic process where the focus was on the collective. Some opted for assemblies where people are divided into small groups—no more than ten to fifteen people—in which everyone reflects on the questions posed by conveners, later to be shared in a plenary-style format. This particular assembly structure, which was used in places such as Mayagüez and Caguas, has revolved around questions that address what is happening in Puerto Rico, what is to be done about the different issues, and how to self-organize. In the case of Mayagüez, those present were asked to join one of ten facilitators who had been chosen from the audience slightly prior to the beginning of the assembly. A note taker was then picked to write down each group's ideas, later to be shared with everyone else. The goal of this assembly format was to allow everyone an opportunity to voice their grievances and ideas—especially those who might be new to political activism.

Other assemblies, such as those in Ponce and Lares, at first chose to do open meetings where those interested in participating had anywhere from two to five minutes—depending on how many people were in attendance—to offer their thoughts on the current situation, or share their concerns and proposed solutions. In these, coordinators requested that people sign up for a turn to speak, as a sort of record keeping to avoid any one person from dominating the discussion, while also holding everyone to preset time limits. Regardless of the model used, the assemblies share common principles of inclusivity, horizontality, and openness.

Organizers also made it clear from the get-go that the assemblies are not a space for political parties to push their agendas but rather for people to present ideas and proposals for transformative social change that emerges from the grass roots. While many of the assemblies have participants with experience in assembly procedures—and the intricate parliamentary process—a significant number of people are new to the scene, making for a space of innovation and experimentation within the democratic exercise.

Even though people's assemblies have just started—and in each town, there are concerns intrinsic to that community—it is already possible to observe which issues are of most importance in the discussions: an intertwining mix of socioeconomic and political concerns.

On the socioeconomic front, on an island where the mounting $124 billion debt and implementation of austerity measures have exacerbated the struggles of working-class and poor people, assembly participants have reiterated many of the popular worries that have been at the forefront of protests in recent years. Fresh on people's minds is the current labor reform, which eliminated rights for newly hired workers and is widely seen as having especially negative consequences for the younger generation, which faces harsher job conditions and thus feels discouraged about staying on the island. Many have also voiced concerns over the crumbling educational system and impact of shutting down schools, not only for children, but for entire communities. For example, at one of the assemblies, Roxana, a sociologist and community organizer, mentioned, "I am very worried about the educational system. We need to demand from the government what is going to happen with our schools. We cannot continue with schools closed in communities that have dire needs; it is not permissible."

Another issue is the privatization of essential services such as health care and utilities, which has been at the center of the government's economic agenda, often imposed through the Fiscal Control Board (FCB), established under the 2016 Puerto Rico Oversight, Management, and Economic Stability Act (PROMESA). Other pressing issues that have emerged in assembly discussions are related to diminishing pensions in light of the government's inability to meet its obligations toward public employees as well as access to safe and affordable housing.

Strongly tied to the socioeconomic issues addressed above, assembly constituents have identified the FCB and illegality of the national debt as two of the most pressing concerns to challenge in the streets and town squares. More than complaining about the burden that austerity measures represent, people at assemblies have made proposals to create citizen accountability boards to demand transparency from the FCB and politicians, and force an audit of the national debt. Voluntary organizations such as the Frente Ciudadano por la Auditoría de la Deuda (Citizens' Front for the Audit of the Debt) have assumed this task and pointed to the unconstitutionality of some of that debt, unfortunately to no avail in relation to the FCB or Puerto Rican government.

Other political concerns include alternatives to traditional political parties and the resolution of the island's colonial situation—themes that echo the protests in July. In the eyes of many assembly participants, the two-party system that dominates national politics—along with politicians' corrupt behavior—have impeded the political process. Traditional political parties in general have failed the people, and lost trust and legitimacy.

There is a consensus among many sectors at the assemblies that the colonial status of Puerto Rico is at the heart of all other matters. The debates over a resolution of the US-PR relationship, be it annexation or secession, have permeated every aspect of political conversation on the island since the end of the Cuban-Spanish-American War in 1898. The current colonial status was further problematized a few years ago after the US Supreme Court ruled in *Commonwealth of Puerto Rico v. Sanchez Valle* (2016) that under the 1952 Constitution, Puerto Rico—as a territory of the United States—cannot claim autonomy, much less sovereignty. This decision broke the spell around the Estado Libre Asociado (Commonwealth) being a sustainable and conclusive status for the island. Many at the assemblies have interpreted the massive street demonstrations as a rising consciousness of this colonial reality and a readiness to move toward decolonization. Given the divisive discussions around the status issue, however, the assemblies have approached this subject with trepidation. Damaris, a participant at the assembly in Mayagüez, advised that "if we want to be inclusive of all sectors, we should be cautious in bringing up the issue of colonialism; not everyone will share that view and will not engage—will not participate." The unity achieved under #RickyRenuncia is seen as still fragile, and there is fear that ideological factions may undermine it.

Almost three months into the assemblies, in an effort to come up with concrete solutions, the overwhelming majority of these bodies—if not all of them—created working groups on a variety of topics ranging from popular education and climate change to alleviating governmental corruption. The agreements and action plans reached by the working groups are later shared in a plenary assembly for a final vote. The recent launch of the Programa Vigilantes Anticorrupción (Anticorruption Vigilante Program), an initiative in conjunction with the Centro Para Una Nueva Gobernanza (Center for a New Governance) to combat government corruption, is perhaps the most noteworthy project to come out of the assemblies so far. Using a secure website, whistle-blowers can confidentially denounce instances of dishonest or illegal behavior by governmental officials.[1] The whistle-blowers are provided with legal as well as mental health counseling, if needed, while the Centro Para Una Nueva Gobernanza investigates and corroborates the submitted information, which will ultimately be made public.

Assemblies are also holding public dialogues that seek to educate communities on a variety of topics such as access to quality and affordable housing, how the national debt and its repayment affects people, and the impact of the reclassification of zoning maps on the island. In some towns, those present at the assemblies have proposed workshops that educate people on critiques of representative democracy and supplied them with the necessary tools to broadly participate in the island's decision-making processes. Other assemblies are proposing the creation of a written resolution collecting people's demands to then be presented to the newly sworn-in governor.

There are clear indicators that people's assemblies wish to be more engaged in decision-making processes that shift from a top-down to a bottom-up model of governance. For instance, Josue at the assembly in Ponce said, "I think that the problem we are facing is that we have a state that does not represent us. . . . We should aim to be part of the decision-making [process], and these assemblies should be a vehicle toward that aim." Furthering this

---

1. "Vigilantes Anticorrupcion," Centro Para Una Nueva Gobernanza, accessed November 4, 2019, https://cpung.org/vigilantes-anticorrupcion.

point, participants in Rincón suggested using the assembly as a stepping-stone to either identify and elect better representatives into the municipal government, or counterbalance the municipal agenda by engaging in oversight and accountability. Others have emphasized that at minimum, we need to cultivate a more active and engaged participatory politics among the populace. And still others have advocated setting in motion a constitutional assembly process to rewrite the current constitution and transform the governing structure from its roots.

Moreover, a consensus has been established regarding the implementation of a Red de Asambleas (network of assemblies), comprised of two members from each assembly. The goal of this network is to work on shared agendas that can have more influence in the national political arena, defend the sovereignty of each assembly, strengthen existing assemblies, and function as an incubator for new ones.

Not lost on people at some of the assemblies is an acknowledgment of the significance of strengthening ties with the Puerto Rican diaspora, which directly or indirectly has suffered the consequences of the socioeconomic and political crisis of the island too. This call to the diaspora is also about seeking support from a community that is seen as fundamental in helping to advocate for the Puerto Rican people through educational campaigns and by using its political power to exert pressure on the US Congress. As Amara at the people's assembly in Lares pointed out, "This local conversation, of the people—it is extremely important for it to have ties with the diaspora; for us to think about the ways in which we can support those in the diaspora who have a desire to help us in alleviating a system that has been designed to dominate."

In recent years, the Puerto Rican community in the United States has gained traction as a political ally and resource to people and movements on the island, as evidenced by its mobilization against PROMESA and the outpouring of support after Hurricane Maria. This connection was further cemented by the number of solidarity demonstrations in July calling for the resignation of Rosselló, and emergence of similar assemblies in cities like Pittsburgh and New York.

It is too soon to know whether this newly acquired power will lead to a radical change in the political structure of the island, and if so, what type of change. What is certain is that the sense of empowerment produced by people's participation in the mass mobilizations has led to a political awakening. People are beginning a process of embracing and experimenting with assemblies, along with the directions it might take them in—that is, empowerment, self-management, and self-determination. The shift from street demonstrations to people's assemblies suggests "the proposal behind the protest"—a principle that challenges those mobilized by grievances to construct their own solutions and present them as alternatives to the current state of affairs. This principle was evident in the groundwork of the Vieques movement (1999-2004), which removed the US Navy's base from the municipal island, and the community work of Casa Pueblo in Adjuntas (1980-ongoing), which has evolved from stopping a mining project into an expansive environmental mission.[2] The rise of people's assemblies across Puerto Rico and their continuous call for the state to respect the people's

2. For more on Vieques, see Katherine McCaffrey, *Military Power and Popular Protest: The U.S. Navy in Vieques, Puerto Rico* (New Brunswick, NJ: Rutgers University Press, 2001). For more on Casa Pueblo, see Alexis Massol González, Edgardo González, Arturo Masson Deyá, Tinti Deyá Diaz, and Tighe Geoghegan, *El Bosque del pueblo, Puerto Rico: Como la lucha antiminera cambio la política forestal desde la base comunitaria* (London: International Institute for Environment and Development, 2006).

voice certainly demonstrates that we are looking at the maturation of a *proyecto de país*: an island-wide project for a new governance.

Quoting the revolutionary independence advocate Ramón Emeterio Betances, Ramón Rodriguez posed a question at the assembly in Ponce: "Why are Puerto Ricans not rebelling?" The assembly responded: "We are here; our moment has come."

*

Jacqueline Villarrubia-Mendoza is an associate professor in the sociology and anthropology department at Colgate University. Her research focuses on Latin American / Caribbean migration to the United States. Jacqueline's work has been published in *Latino Studies*, *Current Sociology*, and the *Journal of Migration and Integration*, among others. Roberto Vélez-Vélez is an associate professor of sociology at SUNY New Paltz. His research has concentrated on the antimilitary movement in Vieques, the intersections between memory, identity, and politics, and US–Latin American political dynamics. Roberto's work has been published in *Mobilization*, *Social Movement Studies*, and the *American Journal of Cultural Sociology*. Both are currently collaborating on a National Science Foundation–funded project related to the emergence of Centros de Apoyo Mutuo (mutual support centers) in the aftermath of Hurricane Maria in Puerto Rico. An earlier version of this piece appeared in *NACLA* on August 29, 2019.

Restoring the Old Ways in the Anishinabe Nation

Shannon Chief in conversation with Laurence Desmarais

For settler colonialism to succeed in what is now called Canada, the land that Indigenous peoples had been living on and caretaking for thousands of years needed to be "cleared out." Starting in the mid-nineteenth century, many governmental policies were designed to erase Indigenous life, such as the planned famines on the plains, weaponizing of smallpox, forced removal of children to Christian residential schools, ignorance of Indigenous knowledge of ecosystem preservation, renaming everything according to settler culture, and more. Most important, Indigenous modes of governance—so foreign to European thought—had to be destroyed. The Canadian government removed Indigenous women from their key political and social roles, banned spiritual gatherings that were crucial to the traditional sociopolitical structures, and regulated and surveiled every person through an "Indian" status system that coerced nomadic peoples into tiny reserves under the authority of a sole agent. The traditional ways of decision making were denied, and an electoral chief and council system were imposed. The Indian Act of 1876, still in effect today, regulates every part of all First Nations communities.

But the attempted eradication of Indigenous peoples by the colonizers was just that: an attempt. Resistance and resilience have taken many forms over the last five hundred years. For some Anishinabeg within so-called Quebec Province, their ways of life on the land and knowledge of their own political traditions have survived through the waves of colonial violence directed at them.[1] *Today, many Anishinabe people are working to restore what was forgotten so that they can govern themselves again. I sat down with Shannon Chief, chosen by her people, the Anishinabeg, to speak publicly as a messenger, in November 2019 to explore these efforts. The following conversation is the result.*

*

LAURENCE DESMARAIS: *I met you in 2015 when a few comrades and I organized a land defense panel in Montreal, and know that you're a prolific advocate for Indigenous rights as well as closely connected to your elders and spirituality. Do you want to start our conversation by introducing yourself in your own words?*

SHANNON CHIEF: I was raised in the Barriere Lake community. I am Anishinabe Algonquin. My parents are both Anishinabe Algonquins. My father comes from Long Point First Nation, which is a little bit north of our territory. My mom was raised in Barriere Lake. A lot of our communities were displaced from their original locations. I have so many relatives in different communities because of my bloodline. My grandmother and her family were from Kitigan Zibi. My grandfather was raised in Baskatong, but lived in Barriere Lake mostly. On my father's side, they are from Long Point

---

1. The Anishinabe people are a large Indigenous group made up of many different singular nations, which in turn stretch from western Quebec to Saskatchewan, from the Great Lakes to the northern boreal forests. The Anishinabemowin language has many dialects and variations, and thus is not unified. This text respects local people's endonym choices. Anishinabe, Anishnabe, Anishinaabe, Anichinabé, Anicinape, Nishnaabe, and so on, are all different accepted spellings. Anishinabe in the plural form is Anishinabeg.

and were also displaced. They were in a place called Sandy Lake; they have always been there, all the way to Wolf Lake.

So growing up with a family connected to different communities, I observed a lot of the issues we're facing. That's the reason why I take part in doing the things that I do today—all of the advocacy and trying to rebuild our own self-governance. I'm doing a lot of research on our history.

We were people who migrated within the territory. We would meet every year to talk about our land and how to take care of it, and we would take that meeting opportunity to report on certain things. We would have what you could call cultural camps. We would canoe our way around the territory. We would know certain places to get fish and beaver, the hunting grounds for moose, where to find medicines and whatnot—the things that we lived on. So we migrated a lot, and that's how we utilized the territory until the Indian Act system displaced and controlled our traditional way of life.

LAURENCE: *Indigenous peoples in Canada were heavily impacted, to put it mildly, by colonization in different ways. Their lands were taken for settlement as well as through resource extraction industries like logging, hydroelectric dams, power plants and lines, mining, and so on. The first paved road to cut across the southern to northern Anishinabe territories in Quebec was finished in the 1940s. The Quebec provincial government created and wrapped a huge 4,860-square-mile park around this road, the Vérendrye Wildlife Reserve, spanning several communities' territories. How did the arrival of the road and strengthening of the colonial policies affect your people and its forms of self-governance?*

SHANNON: Around the 1950s, our people were moved from a place called Barriere Lake to Rapid Lake. The hydropower dam that was built on Barriere Lake flooded the first original village. Parts of this old village and its graveyard are now underwater. Our people didn't have much of a say back then. They would just come in and do what they wanted. These are some of the things that our grandparents shared with us. It's what I have carried from their memories.

We have eleven communities that are recognized under the Indian Act. The government said that it was going to help take care of these communities and the people. Band councils would get certain funding to take care of the people's needs, like education, health, housing, and some jobs. But it never seems enough. The housing never seems enough.

After our communities were settled into Indian Act reserves, a lot of people were forced to live close to one another, and that created problems. Before, when we had the freedom to move places, we stayed in family groups, the way our clan systems are set up. Our clans would take care of what our responsibilities were, and one clan never feuded with another clan. When the government stuck everyone together, social feuding had only began, and people started experiencing dark times with the residential schools and alcoholism. Our way of life with the land and working with one another was disrupted much more in the late 1980s through the political frameworks. Because our people and elders spoke mostly in the language, not all things translated were accurate. So it created misleading ways for those who wanted to extract lumber in a form of an agreement. The decision to take on what was called the Trilateral Agreement [in 1991] separated a lot of families year after year. It practically separated the unity of the whole nation—who we are, as a people. It changed the belief we had of the old ways. The old generation that held all the knowledge didn't fully pass on what should have been passed on to the next generation. Because of a colonized system dominating our Indigenous ways, we now have fewer and fewer language speakers and cultural teachers and history teachers.

LAURENCE: *There has always been resistance to colonialism, and it's inspiring to learn about how people have managed to keep some of their traditional ways, or rescue them, in light of such destruction. Indigenous peoples around the world these days are working internally to bring back their cultural teachings, languages, and traditional modes of governance. Could you tell us about where the Anishinabe nation stands in terms of this resurgence, and what you have been focusing on?*

SHANNON: So when I first started out *Mamwikwek* (with women), it was a movement meant to go around the Anishinabe nation and get to know our people's ways of life to see how we could change things as women. Our people shared a lot of information, like the social disputes that go on in the community, from drugs to family violence, suicide to child displacements. We used to have a specific way of dealing with those disputes under our own self-governance. We always had our own ways of resolving conflicts. We created a balance between the work, the advocacy, and how we took care of the land and animals. Our path as Anishnabeg was interrupted and derailed by the Indigenous and Northern Affairs Canada (INAC) system. We were seen by the white people as having no way to take care of ourselves, since they settled on our land. They didn't understand that we had our own ways. We still have a governing system, which they don't want to see lifted up because it would interrupt their economic interests.

So in the Algonquin Anishinabe nation, we have what we call the old pike constitution. It's always been there since time immemorial. But it has been forgotten; that's how much the Canadian system has imposed on our ways of life. Because of those losses, today there is no sense of who we really are. So we started doing research a couple years back, on the governance, and putting that into writing. We then understood how our people governed themselves back then—from the earth to education to sovereignty.

What did people do when something was going on?... Let's say when there was too much deforestation in one place. How did people move, what were the ethics, and how did they involve everybody? The big law we had was to make sure the information was passed along to everybody. This was how people could then say yes or no, I'm part of it or I don't support it, and importantly, share their concerns. So everybody had a say. The people had a say. And it was the customary chief's responsibility to truthfully speak on what the people wanted. Nowadays, the band chief and council impose what they are going to do. They decide for the people. So after understanding what was going on and shared by the people in our social movements, we are trying to help restore the people's voice by restoring the old ways of our governance.

LAURENCE: *So the Indian Act and band administration are an enforced governance system that destroyed past practices of what could be understood as an Indigenous version of direct democracy. But the council fires are a traditional mode of decision making that is still up and running. You are working to encourage more people to use such tools again. Can you describe the council fires?*

SHANNON: There is a certain structure we have when we make decisions. It was recently created by another wolf clan woman; it hasn't been used yet, but it's for the future. Right now, since as long as I've known, we follow our wampum strings' structure to come up with a decision through the approach of a sharing circle.[2] There are the women, men, and youths in-

---

2. Wampum are an Indigenous traditional object of high value used by many nations across the eastern half of North America. They are weaved with seashell beads of purple and white, and their unique designs are interpreted to teach his-

cluded. The elders sit in as our guidance, ensuring that our constitutional values are within what everyone speaks or suggests. They also make sure there is truth and honesty before they summarize what is said and finally agree to a decision. So the people are decision makers first.

The wampum belts are also important because they play a role in how our governance was shown and how we had our own laws. One wampum belt we carry is about the seven Anishinabe nations. We were a confederacy back then. That is another thing that the government doesn't want us to remember. It was a way that we had more of an inclusive say, and built laws about how the land could be utilized or not. When we worked as nations. It would be nice if our people would go around and share those teachings throughout our communities more. Right now we are unconsciously following the Indian Act like it's the only thing to do. But we still have that blood memory.

LAURENCE: *Can you explain the Algonquin Anishinabe clan system? What role does it play in the governance and social structure?*

SHANNON: In the old days, we had five clans: bear, hoof, wolf, bird, and fish. Here is the story of how that came to be. One day the Creator got all the animals together and said, "You need to create a way of life for the next generation of people that's coming in. These people will need help in structuring their needs and also guidance." So the Creator asked the animals to come together near a little lake. The lake was turned into fat. The Creator

---

torical events or other political matters. They were often exchanged as diplomacy tools, and so the two-row wampum is known as representing the first agreement between an Indigenous nation of Turtle Island and settlers arriving from the Netherlands.

said that any animal who could cross through to the other side would become a clan representative and teach a way of life to its people. For the ones
who couldn't walk through, they would have to walk on the side and go
around. Those animals would become what they call *mandem*, like a spirit
guide. I have the eagle; it's one of the first things I figured out when I was
young, when I was doing a berry-fast lodge. The eagle guides me personally, like for my vision. I get these dreams; that is where I get help from
the eagle. For the clans, five animals made it across. That also explains why
these five types of animals have fatty flesh if you eat them.

Each clan has a specific role. Fish are philosophers; they are most likely
to be teachers. The bear clan, they are the healers and guardians. Like if
you think of a bear, you see it looking around its den all the time. Bears are
protective; they are patrollers. They are also the ones who take care of the
medicine. It's how we get roles and responsibilities—from these animals.
Today they could be doctors or our police. Back then they would be medicine people. The turtles are the ones who make sure that all the clans are
doing what they gotta do. We call them the whip clan [*laughs*]. The bird
clan are the knowledge keepers, and also do a lot of ceremonies with the
hoof. The hoof clan is the one that would traditionally take care of the
gardens, and see through the economic or community development. That
means the hoof clan would be concerned with sharing food and the economy of our hunting—making sure there is not too much overhunting, for
example. The wolves, we are the strategists or warriors, and the land protectors. That's why I am out here, doing the things I am doing. I was trying
to find a way to protect the land. The wolves are fighters for the people.

It is said that if all the clans forgot their roles and responsibilities or ways
of life, the wolves would be the last ones to forget. They have the strongest
memory. So that's the research I do with my clan sisters and elders.

In every clan system, there are also smaller clan groups; for example, inside wolf, you have marten, lynx, and wolverine. There are different kinds of families that can do different things. Each one had a leader animal. The birds are led by the eagle. The fish are led by the turtle. In hoof, it's the moose that is the strongest, but it also has deer and caribou. The five clans are organized in a five-pointed star shape. Each clan works only with two other clans—so that we're not all in each other's faces. It was created that way because there were certain things that just made sense to do. Wolf works well with truth keepers, and also the bears, who make sure we have medicine for us to keep doing our traveling work, and that the information is shared back and forth between bear, turtle, and wolf.

Each clan would have these different roles and responsibilities, and in the middle would be the fire. Back then we would always assemble around a fire, and whatever came out of the deliberations would give us the collective vision on decisions. That's a lot of what Anishinabe self-governance looks like.

LAURENCE: *How do you belong to a clan? Is it through your father or mother?*

SHANNON: That's something that the Anishinabe nation is going through right now. I had to challenge it myself. As a youth, I didn't have all this information. We had to do a lot of research to have it all back. I looked to my mom and aunt to teach me the clan system. I asked my mom one day, "What is your clan?" She said, "I'm wolf." And then I asked, "What is *kokom*'s (grandmother) clan," and she answered, "Wolf." And I guess she had always known what her clan was but never told me [*laughs*]. Oh, so then I understood, you follow your mom's—and because my uncles are also wolf from my kokom's side. So it's matrilineal because your mom is the one who carries you. She carries the life and brings the child from the spirit life to the human life. In our pike bones constitution, we have a bone that is shaped like the womb, with the portal passageway or basically how us women are set up to give life. So the women are the keepers of the clan system. That was the understanding and backing of a matriarchal society.

But before I found this out, I had one person arguing with me that we are to follow our father's clan. I got so puzzled that I went back to ceremony to ask for guidance. When I put my tobacco in the fire, I explained this conflict in my mind that I was experiencing. When I was in ceremony, the second I went in the lodge, the wolf howled. And I was the only one to hear it. I was happy. I explained this at the next opportunity that I had to meet with the person who told me to follow my father's side. This person was upset at me—told me to put that out of my head, like it was enforcing belief on me. More conflicts and disbelief arose, which brought me back to the ceremony to ask for guidance.

LAURENCE: *I've encountered conflicting interpretations of traditional Indigenous governance as being either patriarchal or matriarchal. It's generally agreed on that the Haudenosaunee were matriarchal and matrilineal. But for hunter-gatherer societies like the Anishinabeg, Atikamekw, Eeyou/ Eenou, or Innu nations, many have argued that they were patriarchal. Native women's associations have a lot to confront in their communities, so I know that some Indigenous women would agree that traditional ways don't equate well with contemporary understandings of feminism. Yet it's impossible to talk about what it was really like back then while ignoring how much the last five hundred years have changed everything. Do you think that the supposed common knowledge that Anishinabe clans are patrilineal is a deformation—a legacy of the impact of patriarchy through colonization?*

SHANNON: Yes. When the first settlers arrived, they had the mentality like it's a man's world only. I find this is where it influenced our men from the meetings that they had. I find this is where violence against women also comes from—where men carry that mind-set of having privilege. The understanding we had back then was different. When our people would migrate throughout the territory, the men went ahead of the group. Going ahead was to scout in case of any danger coming so the families and vulnerables were protected. That made men think that men were the leaders and the women would follow. But to us, you go ahead to protect the people, not to direct them about where to go. That's a misconception right there. Truth is, our men were our first protectors, our warriors, our providers, they made good spokespersons and managed political affairs to keep our women safe from outsiders. But we have evolved from that old mind-set and women are doing more what men are capable of doing in this era presently.

So I went back to ceremony and put the same prayer down. I asked for a vision, except I didn't hear but saw something that made my response more believable. My brother at the ceremony was a fire keeper that night. I didn't see anything in the sweat lodge at first. When he opened the door to get the bucket, I saw a big dog head with shiny fur [*laughs*]. I thought it was our dog, Gober, at the time and shouted, "Gober, get out of there!" And my brother was like, "Shannon, what are you doing?" I was really seeing something, you know. So after that I was certain there was nothing to argue about. It was a matrilineal society. That's what ceremony taught me. I'm happy I got the answer. From there, I started advocating for that.

LAURENCE: *Based on how animals relate to one other organically in their ecosystems, the clans teach Anishinabe people how to relate to one another.*

The Anishinabe constitution that you mentioned earlier is another tradi-tional governance tool that is connected to the animal world. Can you ex-plain what it is?

SHANNON: The pike fish normally has twelve bones. Every bone has a shape, and understanding that teaches fundamental concepts and ways for our society. The teachings behind those bones, that is what self-governance was. In the constitution story, the pike is given a thirteenth bone from the sturgeon, and it's shaped like a human being. So we have to con-sider the life of all humanity, as a nation ourselves. Even if we did something on our own, like trying to fully bring back the self-governance system and take away the Indian Act, we would have to consider everyone who lives on our territory—just like we have treaties that were made with wampum belts that said we were going to share the land but not sell it.

LAURENCE: *It seems like respect is at the heart of these ways of belonging and relating. It's striking that these systems rely on internal moral codes that guide people through personal responsibility. I'm wondering how would you apply those constitutional and clan teachings to conflict resolution?*

SHANNON: We think about the issues like, for example, the situation in one of our communities in 2016 when the police shot a youth, or all the children who're being taken away by social services. According to our own self-governance that our committee had discussed, if we had it set up, how would it help the people in these situations? But it needs communication, through the passing or transferring of these knowledges, for it to work. If we looked at how the clan system works and put that into our own form of governance, into our own policing, then the Sûreté du Québec [provin-cial] police force wouldn't be able to come in. And we'd have our own bear clans patrolling and keeping our own people safe—understanding who and where they are coming from. Because the clan system has its own teachings on how to approach such situations. It also applies when it comes to social services or child apprehensions. If our people had gone back to the old ways of how we resolve conflicts, social services wouldn't have to come into our communities or give colonization that much power over our lives, like they had in residential schools. It's still going on today.

We had our own court systems back then. Let's say that a couple was always fighting, and the kids were being affected. We used to bring the couple in front of our elders. Our elders would ask, "What's going on here?" They would listen to both sides and then create a resolution for them. Both people involved would agree to that resolution. We wouldn't need to have other people go into their houses just like that, except for urgent matters, which we barely had any of in those days or spaces. In the old ways, people would always respect what the elders brought in; they didn't fear traditional intervention checking on them. The elders weren't controlling in that sense. They were respected for the long years of experience they had over us. Each had something to offer no matter what.

LAURENCE: *So trust was key?*

SHANNON: Yes. That was the most important thing—the trust we had for each other. And the trust in our self-governance. It was a healthy way. For example, a resolution for that couple could have been to send the guy on a journey for a year to talk to other people and renew his understanding of life. This would have helped him understand his role as a provider in the family and community. The resolution would be to help him reflect on what really matters most in life. Also for the mother, it would help because we women, we won't let go of things when we argue. So she would have to stay close to an elder and be checked on. So she would also have her reflection to do in the resolution and be counseled. Time apart would help focus the needs on her children rather than give her energy on just the man.

LAURENCE: *Would elders from the same clan have led this court panel?*

SHANNON: Yes, it could be elders from the same clan. One clan can work with two other clans. For example, for me, I'm wolf clan, so I can work with turtle and bear. The others, I don't really need to work with directly unless sharing the work done that involves the whole people and the land. This is why our fires are so important; everything passes there, gets resolved there, and we know how to do just about anything that's not colonial [*laughs*].

LAURENCE: *What you are sharing really highlights how both governance and identity are closely linked to the way of life on the land. There are lots of Anishinabeg who live outside the eleven recognized communities. Some live in cities, and some also live out on the land, all year round or almost. I understand that certain families never accepted the INAC system's subjugation, and stayed away from band and council governance, living in aggregations of cabins deep in the woods on their traditional territories. To my knowledge, such a practice on this scale is uncommon within Indigenous nations throughout Quebec. Is living or moving back onto the land an important part of the resurgence process for Anishinabe people?*

SHANNON: Yes, there are more and more. Before, we would live on the reserve and go out camping on traditional lands. We knew which family was responsible for specific places, and we would share our hunting grounds and ask permission to go there for the weekend or to build a cabin there. We'd inform each other. But after the Indian Act caused our families to break apart, resulting in decades of internal feuds, people just had enough of it. Before, if someone lost their spouse, they would move out to the land rather than stay in the same house. It was easier to move on and heal from the grief. But now we have other types of people who decide to move back permanently. They are making their homes out on the land and reclaiming their traditional way of life. For us, we're starting to have practically a village on our territory. And there's more than just ours.

LAURENCE: *A big part of this land is inside what is considered the Verendrye Wildlife Reserve. How do you guys deal with the park authorities?*

SHANNON: Right now our people are really good at challenging them more than ever. We are telling them that we've always lived there. We have sovereign rights to fish and hunt, and we will practice those rights. We are asking for a moratorium on moose hunting, and that requires us to work with other nations. Even though it looked like we were challenging other hunters, it's about getting them to understand that we were always there on this land. When we hunt, we don't take the head for trophy. We use everything. A lot of hunters come in the Verendrye park and don't treat the moose with respect.

LAURENCE: *How are the food resources shared according to the traditional ways? Let's say a moose is harvested. How is the meat distributed?*

SHANNON: It would be through clans. Every clan takes care of each other. If there is less food, we would feed the elders first. And then the ones who can't feed themselves, such as single mothers or vulnerable ill people.

LAURENCE: *Unfortunately not all of the land is viable to live on anymore. What happens if there is a clear-cut and a family can't use their territory anymore? If a family wants to go on the land but their spot is destroyed, how do you manage sharing space?*

SHANNON: That's a good question. My parents had to deal with a lot of deforestation on our land. They were challenging how the industry worked. The logging industry was doing it in ways that involved too much destruction. So there was some conflict with both the industry and band council, which had agreed on some cutting in what it called the Trilateral Agreement. Later on, my family won their case in court, and the band council today is listening more to what families are saying about refusing all tree cutting. Even tree plantations are not so good for the animals. Now it's understood that this section of forest is healing. The moose and animals need sanctuary. If a family says yes to deforestation, so much of it can be gone. Other families will know there is nothing you can find there, except blueberries. So families would go where they know is good to go.

LAURENCE: *So it's OK to go build a cabin anywhere on Anishinabe land for an Anishinabe person?*

SHANNON: No, there are protocols to follow. You have to ask the elders that hold the parts of land first, and then you'd be advised on our way of life out there. Once you have a house in there, you are allowed to hunt. The Anishinabeg were allowed to hunt within the whole territory, but you had to help with the responsibility to notify what was going on in the territory, especially when it involved extractive industries that might interfere with our way of life.

LAURENCE: *That's interesting. Because the Eeyou/Eenou system seems way more strict, adapted after the implementation of the beaver preserves established during the fur trade. The land is divided into traplines, which are strictly delimited spaces regulated by tallymen. A tallyman is a stewardship role normally held by the trapper with the best knowledge among his family of the territory's resources. He decides who can and cannot hunt on their traplines.*

SHANNON: For us, it's more of a collective responsibility. One will stop by your place briefly and say, "OK, I'm going hunting there" and then it's, "OK! Done." But there is accountability, and we make sure we know who, what, and when.

LAURENCE: *That's cool. Having access to good land is so important for healing and connection to culture, food, and so on. I understand Indigenous healing is part of decolonization in a way. My friend Oscar Kistabish, who is an Anicinape elder, talks about how moving back onto his father's territory in the bush was the only way possible for him to feel complete. It gave him the space to practice ceremony. I was wondering if you could talk a bit more about how bringing back those traditional knowledges, spirituality, and ways of life can change how people treat each other?*

SHANNON: We started doing that with people through our gatherings. Slowly talking to everybody about the old ways. People are starting to listen, even families we have had long feuds with. Band chiefs can call community meetings where we pass on knowledge about how it was done back then. It is beginning to repair communication and bring back trust between people. That is how we move people, locally first. Then we will start including other communities like Lac Simon and Dozois. We will be meeting with them and camping out. This is how we bring back the system. Reclamation takes time and effort. We are working on a school curriculum, called Anishnabe Odinewin. We want to implement it in the school, but it's challenging. The only way to do that is to build our own school to start implementing it. It's challenging to get the guys to come together to build something because a lot of them are using [drugs or alcohol]. There is a lot of healing work that still needs to be done just so our people can work together. We are working on that every single day.

LAURENCE: *I don't know if you agree, so please tell me what you think. I have been noticing that families that come from the Barriere Lake community are oftentimes more visible in land defense organizing. I'm wondering if there is a reason that Barriere Lake has a more militant history, compared to other Anishinabe communities we hear less about.*

SHANNON: The communities agree with that too. There are also more wolf clan families in Barriere Lake, compared to other communities. In certain ways, when it comes to sovereignty, they say that Barriere Lake holds the oldest knowledge to lead the way to restore it. When it comes to us being more militant, other community members can see that as violent [*laughs*]. But according to our clan system, our wolf clan and all clans within wolves were the front lines. Humanity is reaching a dangerous point. I feel like our people can't wait another year and another year. Something has to be done now. Now is the time, with climate change endangering all of us each year the longer we wait. We need to mobilize our people locally, regionally, and nationally until we get something from our guided councils, which are the people.

*

Shannon Chief is a wolf clan member of the Anishinabe nation and traditional knowledge keeper. She was raised and has lived on several parts of the Ottawa River Watershed. Laurence Desmarais is a descendant of French settlers, born and raised in Montreal, unceded Kanien'kehá:ka and Anishinabe territories. She navigates between social movements, where she organizes around Indigenous solidarity and noninstitutional art, and academia, where she has been studying settler colonial dynamics in local contexts.

VioMe and Notara 26

TWO NODES IN GREEK SELF-MANAGEMENT

Niko Georgiades

As a response in part to brutal austerity policies, Greece has an abundance of self-managed projects, all pointing toward a new way of life for many. From parallel economies such as the Athens Integral Cooperative, to housing squats such as Spirou Trikoupi 17, to free health care facilities like ADYE serving the Exarcheia community, to independent media collectives like Omnia TV and anarchist information project Radiofragmata, or the House of Women for Empowerment and Emancipation that supports female refugees locked in detention, the list goes on and on. Here I look at two historical yet ongoing examples of self-governance and self-management—the occupied factory of Viomichaniki Metaleftiki (VioMe), and Greece's first refugee and migrant housing squat, Notara 26—based on personal visits to the spaces and many interviews for a series of video documentaries.[1]

---

1. The work done by refugee and migrant squats providing free housing to non-Greeks who've had to flee their homelands due to wars, economics, or the environment have come under extreme threat by the New Democracy—led government, a right-wing party elected into power in 2019. Over 450 refugees/migrants have been removed from their safe and welcoming housing accommodations as government raids evacuated many squats in Athens (Acharnon 22, Jasmine Schools: Second and Fifth School, Hotel Oneiro, Transitio, and Spirou Trikoupi 17) in late August to September 2019. Those removed were sent to detention centers, overcrowded camps (just in time for winter), or deported. It is highly plausible that by the time this book is published, many more housing squats will have been raided and evacuated.

Located on the southeastern outskirts of Greece's second-largest city, Thessaloniki, VioMe is situated within a mass of buildings owned by the multinational company Filkeram-Johnson among miles of abandoned factories. Filkeram-Johnson was the first and largest ceramic tiles producer in Greece before it went bankrupt during the financial crisis of the 2000s and stopped paying its 350 workers in May 2011.

In 2006, meanwhile, a slew of workers at VioMe formed their own union focused directly on workers' rights, and not attached to Filkeram's unions or some of the main types of bureaucratic unionism in Greece, liberal political parties, the state, or the bosses at the factory. Their far more radical union then spearheaded the efforts to occupy the three buildings that they now control. The union had a general assembly in 2012, and called for solidarity from the broader community as well as the other workers who hadn't been paid and were left unemployed by their bankrupt bosses. From that assembly, as a mechanism to garner support from beyond the factory and open VioMe up to society, the Solidarity Initiative was birthed. Organized horizontally through a directly democratic body and created by the workers, the Solidarity Initiative empowered street militants, workers, elders, and the community of growing supporters to discuss the options that the workers had, explore the viability of an occupation, look at what they would produce, and determine how to build the solidarity network needed to successfully self-manage the factory if they were to occupy it. Still to this day, many decisions are made in the Solidarity Initiative's weekly assemblies.

Inspired by similar occupations in Argentina and a restaurant occupation in Athens, these workers and their supporters voted to occupy the factory. From deliberations in both the workers' and Solidarity Initiative assemblies, a collective decision was made that VioMe would produce natural, environmentally friendly cleaning products and vegetable oil soaps, instead of the toxic chemicals that the factory previously manufactured. All the raw materials are biodegradable, and no animal fats are used. This was an important decision because the workers wanted to produce something that was helpful to people, and not harmful to the environment or its users.

To get enough money to buy the raw materials, a large benefit concert was held in Thessaloniki. The workers from the factory and teams of volunteers with the Solidarity Initiative organized the event, which drew in the needed community and financial support to start production. People in the Solidarity Initiative were the first users of the products, and provided networks and avenues to begin distributing the products. VioMe products are now used in households and professional workplaces, such as hotels, restaurants, and hospitals, in Greece and beyond. As Spiros, one of the workers at VioMe and a member of the Solidarity Initiative, put it, "It was a great experience, [a] successful experience, of how rank-and-file daily activists not only can discuss and do propaganda about it but also help and really establish a self-managed project."

In February 2013, a mere six months after the Solidarity Initiative was created, the workers, along with support from the Solidarity Initiative, successfully started running production in the factory. To this day, the workers have full autonomy over all the decisions and operations. They decide what, how, and why to produce specific products, down to the minutest details of packaging and labeling. The workers and their supporters also control who they sell to, and where their products are sold. In this way, the workers ensure that they aren't making products for fascists, or other people or places they don't align with on an ethical basis. Additionally, the workers have complete power over their own working conditions, including who is hired and if someone needs to leave.

Daily democratic self-management is key at VioMe. Every morning, the workers hold an assembly in which they all decide their work plan that day. Their workplace tasks vary individually based on production and distribution needs, where they may be needed most, and even what they themselves feel like doing. The workers rotate tasks and can set their own routines if they like. There is no boss telling another worker what to do. Obviously the work needs to get done, whether that means making or bottling soaps or cleaning detergents, maintenance, paperwork, or inventory. The workers self-manage themselves and get their work done without an authority figure, and with much pride and pleasure.

"We ourselves are working on the production, we do the distribution, even the marketing of our products. Actually, it's us who decide even how we will promote our product," explained Makis, a decades-long worker at VioMe. "The very people who create our products have the power of the production, and moreover, we create our products in a completely different way. We don't create our products for profit; we create them keeping in mind that our products will not harm people or the environment as a whole. We managed, as members of the working class, not to obey orders by the bosses but to make our own orders," he remarked, adding, "and as a comrade once said, 'This factory is a factory that mainly produces dignity,' and that means something, of course."

Beyond the factory, there is a self-managed storefront in Athens, about a five-hour drive away, that sells VioMe's products. The workers in Athens participate in weekly assemblies with the workers in Thessaloniki. Along with the morning assemblies at the Thessaloniki factory, there are further once-a-week assemblies focusing on production and capacity as well as the political happenings in regard to the occupation of the three VioMe buildings. The assemblies are organized horizontally, utilizing directly democratic processes in which everybody is given space to participate; everyone has equal time, equal voice, and one vote. As much as possible, there is no hierarchy. Final decisions are made through consensus in assemblies. When a consensus can't be reached on major decisions, solutions are found in a majority vote.

Discussions happen in the workplace assemblies, organically throughout the factory while working, and within the community. Many of VioMe's larger decisions are made in the weekly assemblies of the Solidarity Initiative so as to ensure that the network beyond just the workers in the factory is fully connected to the self-management of the project. In Thessaloniki, there is also a supporters' assembly; it meets once a year to provide mutual aid and networking via an open web of people from different social movements as well as communities expressing solidarity with self-managed projects.

VioMe is not without its stresses and complications. When tasks aren't completed or responsibilities aren't fulfilled, there isn't a mandated consequence from a boss or manager. The impacts are more personal. Spiros notes that "the main issue is not only voting or deciding about what you do but also being responsible for doing what you have decided." There are times when a person may accept responsibility for a task that they may not have the capability to carry through to completion, and the workers try to deal with this and other issues by discussing them to figure out solutions that benefit all. Arguments happen at times during these conversations, with direct consequences because relationships are essential at VioMe; the workers are like family to each other. If there are serious problems, they have already-determined measures in place within their cooperative agreements, created by the assembly. Consistent communication among workers has been the best way to prevent such negative interactions, though.

The workers have been successful at self-organizing the workplace in such a way that everyone can offer the best that they can do. They utilize their strengths, talents, and knowledge so that the workplace functions well while also improving their own skill sets in other facets of work. For instance, Vangelis, a chemical engineer who now engages in the research and development of new products at VioMe, was at first only a supporter of the struggle, but then he heard that the factory needed someone with a knowledge of chemistry to help create new soaps and products. For over three years, Vangelis has been a part of VioMe, using his specialized knowledge and helping on the production line.

Another dimension of self-management is the need to continually organize against the proposed auction of VioMe's land that happens yearly in the Thessaloniki courts. The land on which the factory sits is still technically owned by Filkeram, so the state puts parcels up for auction to pay off Filkeram's debts. During the annual proceedings, dozens of VioMe supporters fill the hallway within the courthouse where the auctions are held. Two dozen police in full riot gear typically stand in the hall too, or lean against the wall, because the auction procedure takes some time. The people are there in an attempt to physically block the proceedings if someone bids on the VioMe property, but so far, community organizing ahead of the auction has discouraged any would-be bidders.

The significance of the occupied factory goes deeper than just its self-managed production and distribution; VioMe opens up its space to the community and other projects. The factory has become a commons for discussions, workshops, assemblies, theatrical plays, concerts, social gatherings, and film festivals, including cross-movement screenings such as Unicorn Riot's documentary *Black Snake Killaz: A #NoDAPL Story*. Ecological and co-op festivals take place on a regular basis at VioMe, and are all self-managed and horizontally organized.

VioMe has also developed a radical new approach to health care that promotes equal relations between specialists and patients. The Workers Health Care Center, a primary and holistic space with an emphasis on the patient's working conditions, was initiated by the workers. In operation since January 2016, the center was set up in tandem with the Social Solidarity Clinic of Thessaloniki. The autonomous and self-managed center utilizes the concepts of direct democracy and horizontalism in all its relations. The Workers Health Care Center is housed in one of the factory's three occupied buildings. It has a doctors' office, patient room, and medical equipment.

With equality as its focus, the center, which is open one day per week, had over two hundred visits in its first three years of practice. About ten "specialists"—doctors, nurses, and psychotherapists—make up the volunteer health teams that provide integrative health care services free of charge to anyone from the community who comes in. Stressing the importance of how work plays a major role in people's health, the clinic maps the family, relational, and working history of the patient, whom it calls an "incomer," and their relatives. The center combines, connects, and explores the links between the somatic, psychological, and social aspects of life to better understand an incomer's health. Each incomer to the Workers Health Care Center is an active participant in their own treatment. This approach, which emphasizes collaboration, challenges the divisions and hierarchies in typical Western medicine. The center has regular assemblies, and the health care specialists also take part in VioMe's morning assemblies.

The depth and amount of self-management seen directly inside the factory on a day-to-day, hour-to-hour, and even minute-to-minute basis, not to mention outside the factory in the workers' relations to other people and struggles, shows that VioMe is a way of life. As a result, a network of solidarity has formed, weaving through other antiauthoritarian and self-managed projects. From the Solidarity Initiative providing the backbone of community support to the network of assemblies lending solidarity to migrating refugees, to the Workers Health Care Center, to the workers' deep connections to movements such as the effort to stop gold mining in the Skouries, VioMe is an example of what can be done when a self-managed project is allowed to flourish in a tolerant culture.

The ideals of creating a healthy and equal community from the base are not just found among the workers of VioMe, however; they are intertwined throughout various movements. At the height of the refugee crisis of 2015, as hundreds of thousands migrated through Greece and many thousands were in camps, an area in VioMe was used as a distribution and transit point for first aid material and other supplies that were going to the camps from self-organized groups providing mutual aid networks of solidarity to the refugees. This became an important space in Thessaloniki, where many people organized to better handle supporting the people traveling, as the state was ill equipped and at best would lock up refugees in overcrowded camps. Remnants of the significance of this space can still be seen today. An ambulance sits in VioMe's parking lot, where it was dropped off as a donation to Syria, but then stopped and turned back when people tried to take it across the border to Turkey.

Building solidarity with refugees and migrants traveling through and settling in Greece has been a massive undertaking. Many of the people in Greece, facing an extraordinary economic crisis of their own, have self-organized an immense mutual aid network. In the Attiki region alone, where Athens is located, there are approximately forty self-organized social centers, or squats, and about ten are used specifically for housing migrants and refugees. A majority of the refugee housing squats are in the historically antifascist, antiauthoritarian, and anticapitalist neighborhood of Exarch-

eia. These squats are typically in unused state and/or private property occupied by members of the community to provide a space for free housing,
food, health care, clothing, radical discussions, and emotional as well as
psychological support. They help shelter refugees, many of whom have
been forced to flee from their homes due to wars in Iraq, Afghanistan, and
Syria. The squats are self-organized by different autonomous and/or anarchist groups that don't always get along with each other, yet there is an underlying solidarity between them all in the face of attacks by fascist groups
like Golden Dawn and raids by the Greek state—on the increase as of au-
tumn 2019. Security people and basic lookout scouts, for instance, are self-
organized throughout the neighborhood of Exarcheia. The squats, some
of which created the Coordination of Refugee Squats, have also organized
large demonstrations together to demand that the government not raid
their spaces.

Greece's first housing squat for refugees and migrants, Notara 26, sits in
the old Ministry of Labor building on Navarchou Notara Street in Exarcheia. As winter 2015 was coming, and thousands of refugees and migrants
were unhoused, compelled to sleep in the streets or within makeshift
camps in Athens, the antiauthoritarian movement and other anarchist
groups came together in September to occupy the abandoned state building. Since its inception, Notara 26 has housed over eight thousand refugees and migrants from over fifteen countries—for free. Self-managed, this
squat goes above and beyond in delivering mutual aid to people in need. A
common living place, a type of sanctuary, in an accepting neighborhood is
provided for children, the elderly, and men and women from different
backgrounds and religions, escaping the tragedies of war, violence, or the
environment, and speaking many different languages. From September
2015 until March 2016, when the European Union and Turkey made a deal

to close the borders, Notara 26 was mainly used as transit housing. Refugees during that time came for just a few days and then continued north to the borders. After that point, it became more of a home for them.

The organizers inside Notara 26 volunteer to help accommodate people during a transitional time in their life. The refugees and migrants who live in Notara 26 are called "residents," and the volunteers who help are called "solidarians." None of the solidarians live in the building. The residents self-manage the five-floor building along with support from the solidarians. Many of the solidarians have put their personal lives on hold, and some have even come from around the world to provide support.

Directly democratic assemblies are used to make decisions within the building. The assemblies are held in the main room with throngs of residents sitting on couches in a massive circle. Many challenges are dealt with and many are overcome inside Notara 26. Consensus decision making in the assemblies is one of those challenges. To make a collective decision that everybody agrees on can sometimes take many hours, and assemblies in Notara have in the past lasted until three o'clock in the morning.

Because of the large range of languages spoken, translators are key during assemblies. People sometimes must speak one sentence at a time and wait for up to six translators to speak to others near them. Languages such as Farsi, Kurdish, and Arabic are the most common, and some points get lost in translation when going from languages such as Greek or English. The process of translation takes a great deal of time and can be frustrating, so this is a major obstacle—an all-too-familiar one, in fact, for those in Notara.

Another challenge is the learning curve: many of the residents come from different cultures and backgrounds—often from authoritarian or hyperreligious regions—than the solidarians in the self-organized squat and

Exarcheia neighborhood. It can be a culture shock for the residents to suddenly have equal participation in their housing situation and community. After Notara stopped being a transit point, the residents became more comfortable and frequently more involved in the decision making. Yet not everyone wants to participate in the assemblies and decision-making process—even though all are allowed to have a say—and no one is forced to do so.

In order to keep the squat up and running, the residents have established working groups to organize night shifts, cleaning, and cooking. In Notara 26, stretching over the five floors, there is a laundry room, supply room filled with donations, children's playroom, medical doctor's office, showers, and rooms to sleep in. About a hundred residents live in the squat at any given time. The solidarians of Notara 26 bond with the residents when they are there and will go out with them around the community, such as to get food, play sports, or even go to the beach.

Children's drawings adorn the wall in the main assembly area of Notara 26. Cartoon characters, flags, faces, and hand-lettered names are interwoven with vivid picture stories of wars, tanks, blood, and carnage. Notara provides a relatively safe place for the residents and youths to speak about their needs while also giving them access to doctors and psychological services, when desired. Such health care and medical supplies are, in turn, possible due to squat-to-squat solidarity and collaboration with health initiatives like ADYE. Because of the connections between squats, certain services can be offered in different spaces and then shared. For example, a nearby self-managed squat that also provided housing to refugees and migrants, Spirou Trikoupi 17 (until it was raided by police and evacuated on August 26, 2019), had a classroom, allowing the children living at Notara 26 to go to school there.

Indeed, the connections between different squats has proven to be an important factor in keeping the children and residents safe as well. To provide safety for their community, self-managed security squads keep in close touch with other squats multiple times a day to exchange information, share night shifts, and fight back against violent intruders. There are contingencies for the prevention of attacks in Exarcheia when fascists or the state encroaches. Yet acts of violence cannot always be stopped, and in one such instance, in August 2016, Notara 26 was targeted.

About a year after it started, Notara 26 was attacked by fascists, who threw firebombs at the building. Thanks to fast action and proper planning, no injuries resulted that night. The self-managed night shift saved maybe a hundred lives by extinguishing the fire and ushering the residents to safety. The night shift successfully fulfilled the three necessary tasks in the event of a firebombing: put out the fire, alert the residents while getting them out of harm's way, and call the solidarians, who then continue the calls to other volunteers and squats. Although no one was specifically hurt in the August 2016 attack, there was heavy damage to the housing squat and paranoia about another assault lingers. All the supplies in storage were burned, and the first floor and portions of the second floor were badly burned too.

After the fascist attack, Notara 26 was rebuilt in a wave of solidarity reminiscent of its opening. The community of Exarcheia has provided help as well as shown its acceptance of and solidarity for the squat since the beginning. Greeks, internationals, and refugees from all over have come together. Within Exarcheia, a neighborhood with like-minded ideals, Notara 26 has created its own self-governed community with far less discrimination and hierarchy than its residents and the solidarians would experience elsewhere. Solidarians credit the precious relations that emerge through face-to-face conversations, in which people share their various knowledges, joys, sorrows, and everyday life together. Such human interactions continue to serve as motivation, despite the many challenges of mutual aid, solidarity efforts, and security.

Notara 26 was created and occupied while Syriza, a coalition of left-wing political parties, was the ruling party in the Greek Parliament. Even though the political will within Syriza wasn't powerful enough to enact legislation to help squats like Notara 26 and other self-managed projects such as VioMe, many believe that some of those projects were spared being attacked by the state because of the left-leaning parties then in office. In July 2019, this suspicion seemed justified as the New Democracy Party, which won the elections in Greece that year, shut off the electricity at Notara 26 and conducted several raid on squats.

The interconnected web of horizontal, self-organized, and self-managed projects in Greece should not be romanticized. It was in many ways born of necessity and exists against a backdrop of increasing social suffering. At the same time, it offers a tangible alternative to relying on states and capitalism. It requires much effort to practice the ideals of horizontalism, especially in and against the mainstream world, and much time and energy to engage in all sorts of self-directed decision making and actions, in which people must take responsibility for themselves and each other. Yet VioMe and Notara 26, along with the large solidarity network of which they are just two nodes, offer the space to realize and manufacture new possibilities, collectively breathing life into better ways to organize society.

*

Niko Georgiades is one of the founding members of the horizontally organized and self-managed media organization Unicorn Riot. He also serves as the director of operations for WE WIN Institute, a youth-serving organization in Minneapolis, where he has been for over sixteen years. Niko offers thanks to Cindy Milstein for the hard work and vision to make this anthology a reality, and the VioMe workers—namely, Nicole, Spiros, Makis, Vangelis, and Vasillis—and residents and solidarians of Notara 26—especially Giannis, Mimi, and Dionysus—who allowed him and Unicorn Riot into their spaces to document them. He is grateful to the Unicorn Riot family and its supporters. Most of all, he thanks Sindiswa, Dina, and Panos.

guarani–kaiowá

GIVING VOICE TO SOLIDARITY

Cíntia Melo, with translation
by José Renato Fernandes

I first heard about the Guarani-Kaiowá occupation on March 8, 2013, at the women's march in Belo Horizonte, Brazil. I had just run into my ex boyfriend. Still smitten with the love of our recently ended relationship, I invited him to leave the march to go drink a beer and talk. He answered that he couldn't because in a few hours, a new housing occupation would be born.

The occupation didn't have a name yet, but I already imagined what it would be like. It was not the first occupation I had known and taken part in. The metropolitan region of Belo Horizonte had seen an effervescence of housing occupations over the past few years, organized by groups such as the Popular Brigades (now a current of the Socialism and Liberty Party) and Fighting Movement of Neighborhoods, Villas, and Favelas (part of the old Revolutionary Communist Party, now called the Popular Unit) as well as lesser-known social movements.

I wanted to join this new occupation, but the tensions caused by my withering relationship kept me away. Instead I spent an anxious night awaiting news. All the while, I imagined poor families with their meager belongings, children in hand, along with their dogs, cats, plants, and symbols of the affections that people build in life, arriving full of hopes, fears, and the will to fight in this new location. I was already anticipating the script, including the repression, yet was glad to know that my people never stopped trying to meet their own needs, on their own terms.

The new occupation had sprung up on a piece of land abandoned for decades because people viewed the spot as not being in compliance with the "social function" of property ensured by the Brazilian Constitution, which is nicknamed the "Citizens' Constitution." This document was given to us in 1988 to supposedly soothe the pain of many years of dictatorship, and established various types of direct popular participation and land reform. Social movements occupy space, in part, as a reminder to the federal government of its constitutional obligation to challenge private property. This particular terrain had already been cleared of lives, dreams, and projects. It was slated to be exploited by the perverse speculative real estate market, which is stripping thousands and thousands of families of their right to a house.

But various social movements and groups such as the Popular Brigades, Leninist in orientation, know that only collective struggle changes lives. People only have homes, only have their rights validated, through self-organization, self-management, courage, and resistance. Without that, people are dead letters on statist documents.

In the dark of night, the families moved in, setting up their canvas tents, spreading out their belongings, trading welcomes, and starting to cultivate community. The communal kitchen was constructed quickly; people took turns distributing bread and coffee, cooking the beans and rice that would feed the hundreds of people who were there, with a willingness to do anything to claim this space together.

In the first hours of the occupation, the first assembly appeared. The order of events are murky, but somewhere during the evening, before the arrival of the police, a name was chosen: Guarani-Kaiowá.

Guarani-Kaiowá is the name of the traditional Brazilian communities— called indigenous—whose existence in the midwestern region of the country was threatened by the expansionist projects of the national development ideals of the democratic socialist Workers' Party. Between 2012 and 2013, some ethnically Guarani-Kaiowá communities, especially ones located in Pantanal, were at risk of forced eviction, and as an act of solidarity in response, other people started signing Guarani-Kaiowá as their surname to make the point that they were speaking with one voice. Even if people were white-skinned descendants of the Italians or Japanese, or were forcibly brought as enslaved Africans to build the new world in the Americas, everyone was now Brazilian and needed to remember the people who were here before them. Colonization had forged a nation and imposed the Lusitan language, but by adopting the Guarani-Kaiowá name, people proclaimed that they wanted their own history back.

So it was fitting that the new occupation should take up this name as well. Those in power want and need to isolate us. Together, though, when we understand that our struggle is the same, we're stronger; we're seeds originating from the indigenous people, the first Brazilians, collectively creating home on land where the luxury properties of the financial bubble are intended to be erected.

At daybreak, the police arrived, yet they were met by a commune. People defied the powers of the state and capital not only because they needed housing but also because of the bonds of love and solidarity developed between them by reclaiming this terrain. The police surrounded the land, engaged with those it deemed leaders, threatened them with imprisonment, then called in the shock troops and tried to destroy the occupation. The people stood their ground—so much so, they're still there as of 2019.

The initial few days of a housing occupation are always remarkable experiences, and so I decided to go to Guarani-Kaiowá after all, notwithstanding my own personal heartbreak. That's when I heard the first rules

from one woman: "Look, girl, everyone here has to participate. We decide
our destiny for ourselves. The assemblies all happen beneath that tree, and
we discuss the future together. In here, the law of the powerful has no
worth. And you know, men cannot beat women. If they do so, they have
to leave."

The Guarani-Kaiowá assemblies, like ones at similar recent land occupations, were open to participation from both residents and supporters. But
especially during the first days, all the residents were strongly encouraged
to join in the assemblies, considering that the initial period is decisive for
the permanence of any squat. Given that Brazil at this time already had a
strong tradition of mass movements, and most were related to the right to
adequate housing, many points on the assemblies' agenda already came
with a known, trusted background, including lots of prior deliberations and
practices from other occupations that could be built on here. The same
was true for various strategies and tactics, which had been widely applied
across movements. So leaders who had participated in other land occupations, along with lawyers, supplied the first Guarani-Kaiowá assemblies
with well-established know-how from other actions. The new community,
of course, then made its own decisions, but often without need of too much
discussion. Still, everyone who wanted to debate ideas or put forward other
perspectives was welcome to do so.

The first assemblies (during the first months) usually lasted about three
hours to ensure broad participation and the creation of bonds. To maximize
the number of people in attendance, especially when urgent decisions
were going to be debated, the day or even some hours before an assembly,
a group of residents and supporters would go from house to house inviting
people to come. Pamphlets, loudspeakers, and fireworks were also used to
announce the assemblies.

Consensus was sought during assemblies, yet when there were differing viewpoints, those present offered various opinions, trying to exhaust all the avenues for achieving agreement. If and when it became clear that consensus was not possible, people turned to voting, almost always by the visual method of residents raising their hands. As part of this process, it was common practice to use facilitators and note takers for discussions and decisions. While both roles were voluntary and rotated, they weren't decided on in advance. Instead, facilitators and note takers were chosen at the assemblies, but only when there was a need for them.

During the first weeks of Guarani-Kaiowá, the need to define collective logistics was more pressing than it would be later, after the community had established itself, so the assemblies debated political orientations along with tactics and strategies of direct action and resistance. Assemblies saw to the organization of daily life too, such as volunteer roles and shifts for community needs like security, the communal kitchen, and childcare as well as infrastructure for communication with the outside world, agitprop, legal actions, and so on. Moreover, the assemblies decided how to raise funds, who would be responsible for the management of these monies, and how those funds should be spent. In this way, residents ensured the sustainability of their community, through communal support, until their homes were built and people were literally on solid ground.

When I first showed up with my social movement companions, all well-intentioned militants, none of us rich, nor wanting to control things, we were welcomed to join in as supporters. But vanguardist political groups also insisted on being there, maneuvering for prominent spots during the assemblies. I could see some of the same leaders and faces in the crowd as at past occupations—the same whiter, better-dressed people than those who had actually squatted and now lived on this land. All of us already had homes, and good ones, in areas of the city where the police do not come with rifles at the ready. I was one of those people too.

Don't misunderstand me; my friends and I didn't want to appropriate the struggle of others. Yet we had a fragile comprehension of the real meaning of autonomy and self-management. And our presence, alongside the more hierarchically oriented Marxist-Leninist groups, at times inadvertently created unhealthy power dynamics within assemblies.

So I tried to be humble by observing what was going on and only participating in ways that the new residents suggested. I kept walking around, watching the children running about happily, marveling at the improvised bathrooms, and ending up under the tree that was home to the assemblies—such a radically different space than what our statist democracy offers us elsewhere.

I talked with the people who had occupied the land. Someone asked me to bring donations. They lacked everything: construction materials, cleaning products, food, and even money. I spoke with another woman, who had one child in tow and was visibly pregnant: "Now this is our home. Where I came from before, my whole payment from cleaning jobs was spent on rent for a single-room shack with my three kids. Now this home I'm building will be ours."

An assembly began. The leafy tree received the residents. I saw about a hundred people organized in a circle. I saw these words on T-shirts and banners: "If living is a privilege, occupying is a right." I heard the cries of war: "We fight and we won't wilt, until our homes are built!" I heard the familiar catchphrase of the Popular Brigades: "Free homeland! We will win!"

The few available seats were mostly being used by older people. Some people sat on the ground, while most stood up, listening attentively and excited to participate. Although it was still summer in Brazil, the evening was windy and not especially warm. As this was in the early days, before the houses were constructed, we were surrounded by nature. A large majority of the assembly was composed of women, some of them holding their children, but dozens of kids were playing next to the assembly too, starting to learn how to be part of a true *comuna* (commune). Most of the residents were racialized; in terms of how Brazilians categorize race, they would call themselves "black," but in the US or Canadian context, the term "person of color" would likely be applied to them.

People shared and listened to each other, relating everything from their worries and feelings to their ideas and visions. The first speeches were marked by deep emotions. Gradually, the urgency of setting up the community compelled people to turn to more pragmatic concerns. For instance, they began to activate their networks so as to provide Guarani-Kaiowá with more support, such as donations, political aid, and outreach. The need for physical spaces for nurturing community cohesiveness was also discussed, and in the first few months, social events like parties and cultural activities were crucial in forging friendship and solidarity. Assemblies took place weekly under this same tree, with additional ones when emergencies arose.

To this day, consensus is still always sought, and decisions are legitimized by popular participation in the assemblies, which are now basically permanent and even still meeting weekly depending on the context. There is no rigid or written code about how the assemblies work, nor is there a rigid or bureaucratic leadership structure, so the procedures can change over time according to the circumstances. Yet the informal practices within the initial assemblies have now basically become tradition. Recent assemblies have typically lasted less than an hour. Since nowadays a shared cultural, political, and social identity between the residents is firmly entrenched, and the occupation itself is experiencing relative tranquility in terms of being able to stay put, the assembly conversations can be much lighter and shorter. Residents bring up subjects concerning their daily organizing efforts or everyday life in common, for example, and these issues are freely explored. Although the regular assemblies are usually not crowded, participation swells when there is an imminent eviction threat, recent police intervention, or the need to plan a direct action.

On occasion these days, the assemblies can be a bit longer for another reason: to talk about and decide on logistics for social events. In June 2019, for instance, the community organized a solidarity party, similar to a collective baby shower, to raise funds for some pregnant comrades, focusing on money for diapers, clothing, and other infant needs. This solidarity party didn't take place within Guarani-Kaiowá itself but rather at another squat called Kasa Invisível (Invisible House), an anarchist social center and important partner in various housing occupations in Belo Horizonte. The baby shower was open to the public, not only residents or supporters of Guarani-Kaiowá.

Guarani-Kaiowá's own birth in March 2013 was the first breath of what would become a popular insurrection throughout Brazil by June of that year, and many other occupations would be born too, such as the enormous Isidora. These urban occupations coupled with the youths of the Movimento Passe Livre fighting for free and high-quality public transport for all, the feminists agitating for safe and free abortion as well as an end to femicide, the attempts at creating free media, and the peasant movements had all been stirring in Brazil for a long time. Yet the public demonstrations in numerous cities, known as the June Journeys, set the tone that Guarani-Kaiowá helped to start: we want to own our history.

The Guarani-Kaiowá community has become stronger over the years.

Several times since 2013, the state has tried to back the interests of the supposed property owners of Guarani-Kaiowá's land through police raids, legal actions, and eviction attempts. A group of lawyers with socialist ideals has always came to the aid of the community—an essential component of its self-defense. But Guarani-Kaiowá residents were also able to defend themselves through marches, direct actions, road blockades, and an occupation of the public utility company's head offices. In this way, residents imposed their own agenda and gained infrastructure, such as water and electricity.

Furthermore, through joint efforts and collective decision making, the community has been able to thrive, building its own spaces. Residents, of course, autonomously built all their own homes, and Guarani-Kaiowá now has a social center, streets, and numerous communal activities. With the help of a network of lawyers, architects, sociologists, and others—all organized more or less horizontally—the community received the technical support necessary to develop its own neighborhood. This collaboration was so successful that in 2013, the São Paulo Architecture Biennial selected Guarani-Kaiowá occupation's urban planning project as an example of innovative practice.

As well, soon after the initial occupation, various political movements set aside their differences to celebrate this self-formed community, knowing it was already victorious, no matter what. And so militants, people with expertise, and other nonresidents set up a support network for the island of resistance called Guarani-Kaiowá. Anarchists, organized as the Popular Anarchist Committee of Minas Gerais as well as the Land and Autonomy Front (today called the Base Organization Movement), became more engaged in the occupation, along with the populace and Popular Brigades, and all have actively joined in the community's political steering committees, now six years old. In turn, the residents of Guarani-Kaiowá have housed projects, including Black Land, one of the most important anarchist convergences in Brazil, where for three days anarchists and libertarians from around the entire country gather to debate, sing, dance, build, learn, and teach, on topics ranging from self-defense strategies, feminism, and self-management, to DIY culture, agroecology, and veganism.

In addition to assemblies within specific squats like Guarani-Kaiowá, Belo Horizonte has a steering committee for all the occupations. This body is supposed to be a permanent forum or committee, but it goes through peaks of activity and has little formal structure. From time to time, the committee goes completely dormant, but when needed, it springs back to life. It is made up of residents from diverse occupations, participants in various social movements and political organizations, professionals (such as lawyers, architects, and sociologists), church members (mainly Catholic), and people affiliated with universities. The meetings are held in various places, with the aim of expanding and connecting struggles around the city as well as generating momentum for popular mobilizations when there's urgent need. One of the main motivations for the committee to actually meet, in fact, is when an occupation is facing an imminent forced eviction.

Significantly, though, the fight for housing in Belo Horizonte, beginning with the early milestone of the Dandara occupation in 2009, has ensured homes for tens of thousands of people through their own direct action. The popular movements, including Guarani-Kaiowá, have been responsible for constructing more housing units over the last decade than the state itself.

Today, as I write, we walk in fear and face dark times in Brazil. Not that the government ever was a true friend of the people, but now a clearly fascist president, Jair Bolsonaro, occupies the palace. We have no choice, of course: we must continue to fight. Guarani-Kaiowá is dynamic proof that the struggle is not only worth it but also life affirming. It is space not merely against fascism; it is tangible evidence of our ability to create our own spaces of dreaming, courage, solidarity, and community life. And love.

*

Cíntia Melo is an anarchist lawyer and writer, with a master's degree in architecture and urbanism. She is Brazilian, involved with fights for the right to housing, transport, and the city as well as gender equality. She has been involved with political organizations and social movements, living and fighting in different countries, such as Brazil, Argentina, and the United States. Special thanks to José Renato Fernandes, the comrade who translated this piece from Portuguese to English. His professional contact is jrfskreemer@gmail.com.

Christiania

A FREE CITY IN THE CITY OF COPENHAGEN

Asbjørn Nielsen

The remains of fortifications left over from sixteenth- and seventeenth-century wars between Denmark and Sweden sit on the outskirts of central Copenhagen. Big earthen ramparts and moats surround a stretch of land spanning seven acres. Made up of housing barracks, stables, and weapons factories, the area was abandoned in the late 1960s, yet today offers a startling contrast to its martial past.

When the guns and uniforms moved out, immigrants from Copenhagen's hippie community moved in. Artists, left-wing radicals, dreamers, and people of all kinds squatted the area, gradually setting down roots along the ramparts. The cannons were replaced with trees, and the moats were eventually filled with more than a hundred species of birds, which now thrive in the green oasis.

Consisting of about eight hundred people—two hundred of them children—Christiania is today one of Copenhagen's main tourist attractions, drawing more than a million visitors a year from around the world. It is a declared, if not totally autonomous, city by its own constitution, consensus-based democratic structure, and unique blend of urban and village-based community.

During its more than forty years, Christiania has evolved to both function independently from and in symbiosis with capitalist society, and most important, has managed to thrive, presenting living proof that human beings and solidarity can indeed be set above the demands of profit and accumulation.

Through interviews and analysis, I take a look at some of the ways in which consensus and autonomy are perceived as well as practiced by the inhabitants of Christiania. I also discuss how the free town interacts and negotiates with the surrounding city and Danish state.

From Army Base to Utopian Village

Jørgen has lived in Christiania since its inception and raised several children here. Today he lives on a small farm named Autogena on the borders of the ramparts. Lying close to the water, the house is more than three hundred years old, and originally served as a munitions depot and barracks for the local garrison. With a view to the moat and nearby trees, nature is close by, and only the sound of birds and bikes passing by disturbs the silence, which is an odd but crucial luxury if one considers how the noisy rush of the city is less than a kilometer away. The farm houses twelve people in a collective, including Jørgen's daughter Marie, and along with many other homes, is a building block of Christiania's fourteen neighborhoods. These neighborhoods include large apartment buildings, small farming communities, businesses, and music venues as well as one of the largest green areas in all of Copenhagen.

Jørgen works as a gardener and craftsperson, employed by the Christiania community to oversee the maintenance of the historic fortifications, forests, and moats. Walking around, he has a story about each house and area, and a broad knowledge about the history of Christiania.

"Before a big public storm on the area in 1971," Jørgen reminisces, "lots of people had already started seeping in and settling in the old army barracks. The facilities used to house the army's horse-drawn artillery, which was antiquated [and hence abandoned] in the 1940s, when the modern

German army swept across Europe and demonstrated the efficiency of motorized guns."

He explains that "from the beginning, we had a general agreement about maintaining a decentralized structure and consensus in decision-making processes. Important matters should be discussed and decided in their respective neighborhoods and areas whenever possible. Starting from this we divided the space into ten different areas, which today have grown into fourteen. Everything is to be decided on a local level, and only if a decision cannot be made or something concerns others, then it is taken to a larger assembly from the neighborhood or the big common meeting, which functions as the highest decision-making body in Christiania."

As Jørgen further describes, "Each inhabitant pays a fixed amount of rent as well as thirty Danish crowns for every square meter they inhabit. We have developed a system that allows people to purchase a certain amount of electricity and water according to what they need, thus reducing overusage. In each area, a treasurer is elected to oversee the collection of rent and manage the finances within each given neighborhood."

For its first eight years, Christiania attracted a growing number of vulnerable individuals with nowhere else to go or hoping for a fresh start. By the end of the 1970s, however, another arrival became a fundamental threat to the community. The introduction of heroin had a massive impact, with hundreds quickly becoming addicted. This led to what became known as the "junk blockade," where those who wished to quit the drug were offered help, and the community instituted a total ban on hard drugs, leading to the expulsion of a large part of the population that was unable or unwilling to undergo detox. The current archivist and lore keeper of Christiania is Ole Lykke, who arrived in the free town right when the blockade began and a rescue operation to save the community was launched.

"When I moved here in 1979," says Ole, "the place looked sad. I had earlier been offered [the chance] to live here, but had refused due to the state of the place. People were moving out in droves, and the junkies took up more and more room. Then the blockade came. People took action and dedicated themselves full time to eliminating the shit from Christiania. I was asked to document the process through pictures, and after a week, I got caught up in the movement and helped to form a collective known as Ararat on the third floor of the building known as the Arch of Peace, where most of the junkies had lived. The place was so bad that it even had a café in which a free needle and heroin were offered to beginners."

Ole notes that "when the blockade was over, no more than twenty residents remained in the huge building, and it only had three functional toilets. We saved it eventually, and it was an amazing thing to see two hundred people working day and night for forty days to put the place back in order."

Today Ole manages the archive, which is located in the very building where the junk blockade started. Encompassing the entire history of Christiania, the archive's shelves line the walls from top to bottom, stacked with neatly ordered rows of newspaper clippings, books, slides, tapes, and CDs containing a life's worth of effort. The material is all neatly cataloged, ready for someone to "take up the mantle and write the magnus opus of Christiania's history," as Ole remarks—a monumental task that has yet to be attempted.

Between the early 1980s and today, Christiania again became a beacon of hope with dozens of cooperative businesses, stores, and concert venues opening. At the same time, the still-tolerated cannabis trade attracted criminal groups such as the aptly named motorcycle gang Bullshit, which eventually disbanded after Hells Angels' members took over the drug trade in Christiania and assassinated the leaders of the rival gang.

From the Autogena farm, Jørgen and Marie enjoy a view of the houses, often built according to the inhabitants' needs and desires, near the waterfront. Looking across Christiania's lake, Jørgen starts to share some of his wealth of knowledge about their residents, many of whom he's known since his youth. "The low building that you see on pontons by the edge of the lake was built by a guy named Klaus," Jørgen says, gesturing toward a two-story building that, true enough, is floating on the water's surface. "Being a metal worker, he built the frames and then added to it over the years. The low height of the building is deliberate since he and his wife aren't tall, so they reduced the average height of the rooms and door frames by thirty centimeters."

Pointing to a nearby house that bears an uncanny resemblance to a flying saucer, Jørgen describes the first owner in detail, along with his later flight after having been involved with and impregnating several women in the neighborhood.

All the buildings not connected to Christiania's homebuilt sewage system have a bio-organic system from different layers of gravel and sand that filters all waste into breathable air and water, which then floats back into the surrounding moats. This system is checked yearly by Copenhagen's environmental authorities and so far functions beyond all expectations. The engineers of the system have even been asked to demonstrate and construct similar ones in Cojimar, Cuba, with the help of the Danish-Cuban friendship association.

Walking down the road from Autogena and passing a woman driving a small scooter with a cart trailing behind it, Jørgen explains, "This is our resident social worker employed by the community. She takes care of the ones who need it as an investment in the community. More often than not this includes people with alcohol-related problems. Of course one tries to help, but most refuse help, and Christiania is sufficiently inspired by a hedonistic philosophy to allow people to continue an addiction that does not include hard drugs, but at the same time also sees it as an investment to keep them alive and offer aid should they want it. People who live here do the things they want to do simply based on their need to do it, even if it is harmful to themselves, like drinking or smoking too much."

This attitude underscores that within this free city, as Jørgen puts it, "people believe in what makes sense to them" in all spheres of life, including faith. "We aren't an exclusively atheist community," Jørgen says. "Take the priest, for example. John is a carpenter by trade and decided to help found the church because he thought there was a need for it, and he learned the tasks of being a priest as he went along without being officially ordained." Functioning as both independent and free, and occupying a small house near the center of the community, the church attracts a small but loyal congregation. Several Buddhists also make Christiania home, as evidenced by the presence of a small stupa near the inner ramparts. "Everyone has a place here," Jørgen affirms, "if they give space to others as well."

Christiania is in many ways a safe haven for people who otherwise wouldn't fit into the rest of society or don't wish to fit in. There is a higher degree of tolerance for people regardless of their social standing, or whether they'll do things or cause problems that in mainstream society would compel people to call the police. "There is a willingness here to solve matters in a way that everyone can agree on and that allows everyone to live the way that makes sense to them, though without causing harm to others," Jørgen remarks. "If my neighbor, for example, gets absurdly drunk and starts causing trouble for others, I first try to speak with them, and if it doesn't work, I take it up at the local-area meeting, which then tries to solve it or call the social worker in order to help my neighbor."

A small but visible illustration of this "do what makes sense for you" philosophy is the miniature sailing ships spread throughout the canals around Christiania. Beautifully carved and painted, the small vessels are tied to anchors that allow them to move in eight-shaped patterns. "These ships are manufactured by several people of Greenlandish decent," Jørgen says, pointing to a nearby ship making its way across the moat, its sails filled with a fresh breeze. "They make them because they enjoy it, and not because anyone told them to or took a decision that they should be there," he comments, adding, "Not for any practical reason, but because they like the aesthetics and craft that goes into them."

Though seemingly benign, this philosophy is reflected throughout Christiania and is fundamental to how it constitutes more than just a physical space governed differently from the rest of society. The very sensibility of doing the things you want to do because they make sense for you, and the community rewarding and facilitating this, is something that is frequently overlooked yet contributes to the overall feeling of self-determination in this place.

"The people like me who enjoy working with their hands in the soil, they help maintain the organic balance and preserve the green areas, such as the forests, ramparts, and moats. Those who want to build or make art do that. Those who want to do finances or music do that," he explains, observing that "all are part of what makes this place unique and why we call it home. The enormous cultural life here is great, and as a community, it is just the right size, with just the right amount of people and right amount of nature. We're what used to be the average size of an old parish, and like that, we have sufficient intelligence, knowledge, and skills to function as a small community in itself."

Jørgen continues, mentioning that "there is a large amount of artists and musicians living in Christiania compared to other places—many of whom have made it their way of making a living. Alongside doing what you love, we value it being a part of our lives where we live. It is something that has been lost in most places, where home and work are divided into mentally and physically separated spheres. In most places, it is illegal to have an overlap between work and living space, thus making whole areas dead and abandoned for half the day, only to transit through, leaving either work or the home deserted. It takes away the opportunity for people to have a way of living besides that which society allows. Home or work becomes a place where you go and just are while waiting to go to the other spot; it takes away inspiration and creativity. Imagine the life it would bring if work was part of how and where you lived? It used to be like this, but we have all but forgotten it. In Christiania, we have worked to reestablish and keep it as a way of life, to make it a city adapted to humans and not us being fit into preconstructed boxes for optimal efficiency."

Christiania inherited a "preconstructed box" in terms of the physical infrastructure, but has managed to transform it in various ways, such as the ongoing renovations of the five-story army barracks as well as cleanup operations in areas contaminated by the past military inhabitants.

In a central building surrounding a courtyard, Jørgen and Marie point out the places where several meters of surface earth have been removed and replaced with imported dirt. "This used to be an old war laboratory. Here the military manufactured chemicals and poison gas for use in war, and experimented on animals and people," says Jørgen. "It looks idyllic now, but the ground is chock-full of poisons that have seeped down with the rain. The people who first tried to dig here had to be hospitalized because of ugly rashes and burns from stuff left in the ground. All the dirt here was changed out so we could plant grass and trees, and ensure the safety of the children living here. In many other places, it is still dangerous to dig more than a meter down."

One of the oldest buildings constructed after the founding of the community houses a public bathhouse. Anyone living in or invited to Christiania can enjoy a shower and a mixed sauna. Like in many ancient societies, the bathhouse is a gathering place. As Marie describes it, the bathhouse "is a public place for people here, but many others come to use it. People usually gather here for philosophical discussions, and you can meet all kinds people here—from hard-boiled bike gang members to the softest hippie. The general rule is that all topics are up for discussion. The only thing not allowed are bad vibes. People come here to relax, and anyone is allowed a veto and to demand calm if a discussion becomes too heated and disturbs others. Of course people also smoke a lot of weed here, but only if no children are present, in which case all smoking ceases."

There are, in fact, many children living in Christiania. Recently, a few documentaries have aired on national television showing what it was like to grow up here in the early days, and several people attested to "having seen too much, too early" in this fluid society where children were given a freedom not imagined by others of their age living elsewhere in Denmark. Certainly no single story can encompass everyone's upbringing in this free city, but things often weren't rosy for kids, and as such, it's somewhat taboo to even talk about it.

Marie was born and raised in Christiania. "You grow up in an enormously strong and safe community here," she said of her experience. "You go to the same nursery, the same school, and you know each other's parents; it's almost like being siblings. As you grow older, you start to perceive the bubble, and it dawns on you that the world is bigger despite Christiania being one of the best places for a kid to grow up. Attending school and gymnasium outside the bubble, you also meet with a lot of prejudices, like that the whole community [is supposedly] addicted to weed, and it is nothing but a place for drugs and drug dealers shooting each other. Eventually you realize the beauty of this community, but it takes venturing outside to perceive it."

Autonomy and the Surrounding Society

Since its inception, Christiania has been a topic of debate for successive Danish governments and the city of Copenhagen. Proposals to either forcefully evict or normalize the community have been offered and abandoned. The issue wasn't resolved until 2012, when the neighborhood went from being a large-scale illegal squat to assuming collective ownership of the property. In exchange, Christiania accepted concessions such as having to take out a loan and purchase the area from the state as well as working with the city of Copenhagen on certain social issues.

One of the things that has allowed Christiania to function as an autonomous community for as long as it has is its strong institutions, all of which meet regularly to discuss ways to assist and complement each other. The free city has its own self-constructed sewage system, self-run nurseries and kindergartens, social workers, cooperatives, and a wealth of different musical venues and shops that contribute to Christiania's own economy by providing services and attracting customers from the surrounding society.

The surrounding society is in fact indispensable since Christiania is by no means self-sufficient, being located in the middle of a large urban center. Unlike other autonomous communities that are often found in remote or rural areas, the free city in Copenhagen has always functioned in symbiosis with the Danish capital. Yet it has continued to do so without compromising its founding values or strong local sense of community. One knows immediately on entering Christiania that one has "left" Copenhagen and is in a more autonomous space, from the sign at the entrance that says "You are now leaving the EU [European Union]" to the vibrant street life. Passing from the neighborhood of Christianshavn into Christiania, one instantly notices the complete absence of cars. Instead bikes, people on foot, and dogs dominate the paths that wind between tall trees and broad green areas. The noise of a metropolis is replaced in Christiania by music and conversations from cafés and street corners. Brightly colored stands sell food and drink, homemade instruments and trinkets, and cannabis and hashish of all types and sizes. Unlike the surrounding streets of Copenhagen, you see people nodding and smiling at each other, most knowing each other as neighbors and coworkers.

Elin has lived in Christiania for the past decade. "When I go down for a coffee or to use the local free shop, there will always be someone who I have to say hello to, who greets me or at least gives a friendly nod. I feel completely safe here, and considering that this is an urban area, children run almost everywhere playing with minimal supervision. In this way Christiania is much like a village in a big city," observes Elin.

Autonomy in a community like this is hard to pinpoint in the larger picture, yet it is frequently evident in the small details of everyday life.

As Elin puts it, "One has to relate to and consider more things than if one was living in a regular building complex. We maintain the buildings ourselves, and so people like me sign up for a committee with members from the different local areas, and if something new is to be built, we do it ourselves or find someone to do it, or we figure out how to work things out with the Copenhagen government and Danish state. For example, a bike path goes through Christiania. We have to renovate it, but how will we do that? Some people want there to be bumps for the safety of children, and others wish it to be a fast route for commuters. We're discussing these things and trying to reach a consensus. Autonomy here is continuously being negotiated and changed depending on the circumstances or the people participating. We are formally under Danish law, but we also have our own constitution that people living here and visiting must adhere to. Sometimes that conflicts with Danish law, and some people who were evicted from here for violating that code have been allowed by the Copenhagen government to move back in again. At other times, such legalistic conflicts between Christiania and the state are not a problem."

Just as autonomy in Christiania is about active participation, it is also about choosing your battles and not fighting for everything at the same time. Some issues are harder to resolve or deal with than others.

A concrete illustration of this is the passageway within Christiania known as "Pusher Street," where cannabis is sold openly in defiance of the Danish laws banning it as an illegal substance. Located in the center of Christiania's main street, and surrounded by a jazz club, bakery, and residential buildings, several stalls line the street and offer every kind of cannabis imaginable. There is frequently a delicate balance between those Pusher Street dealers who live and work in Christiania and the harder criminal elements and organized gangs that sell there too, given their reputations for violence. While both sets of dealers often actively oppose police incursions and raids, conflicts between them have arisen, and Christiania has been the scene of several lethal shootings and disputes, prompting immediate action from the free town through complete shutdowns of the cannabis trade. This decision was taken in order to minimize violence and clearly state that it has no place in the community as well as limit outside responses from state authorities and police.

Clear boundaries and community ground rules, determined by consensus, are in place for selling cannabis. No fights between dealers or rival gangs are allowed. No one is permitted to use weapons, nor is there any tolerance for masks intended to conceal the identity of dealers. And so in sharp contrast to shootings between rival gangs competing for a piece of the highly lucrative cannabis market in Copenhagen, a stable peace generally exists within Christiania.

Just as important as the ground rules for selling cannabis, however, is the free town's no-tolerance policy for hard drugs, which if violated, carries with it immediate expulsion. Several people work daily in dialogue committees that maintain active communication with the dealers on Pusher Street and the police, without giving harmful information to either, but aiming to keep the peace and uphold the safety of the community.

Marie describes it this way: "Christiania is our home, and there have been moments when we have taken time to put things on a break, and discuss internally what we want it to be and how we want things to be run. One thing we don't want is for fear and forces from outside to take that power away from us."

Christiania is also home to more than four hundred jobs of different varieties. Some are found in the roughly thirty small businesses, while still others are part of the administration and general maintenance of the moats, forests, buildings, and nature reserve that make up the former army base. These jobs include gardeners, carpenters, masons, and teachers, among others. Salaries are paid in Christiania's own currency, which is exchangeable for goods and services within the community.

In addition to its own currency, the city of Christiania offers loans for general maintenance or large-scale projects. Inhabitants can borrow the money from their own community instead of paying interest to outside banks, which would likely reject them anyway. Similarly, extra-large projects can be funded through Christiania taking out a bank loan and functioning as a middleperson, and then the borrowers pay back Christiania. Such practices help to reduce the power of banks to charge outrageous interest on loans to individuals and insures a payback of the loan, since people are in essence investing in and funding their own community. Though the interest on loans is not decreased, having the community as a buffer allows for more flexibility in paying back when one is able to as well as providing a stronger security than could be put up by individuals.

While Christiania retains most of the services and structures of an independent commune, and as such is more autonomous than any other Danish municipality, its self-organization has limits and is increasingly threatened.

"When we bought this place from the state, the agreement was that we would be able to mind our own affairs in peace. With private property and populated buildings, however, came the laws regulating it," bemoans Jørgen. "Now almost ten years later, we are up to our asses in Danish laws and regulations. We can hardly move an inch without having to ask permission."

In this sense, although secure against eviction, Christiania is compelled to grapple with a dual-edged sword. Its agreement with the state and decision to take private ownership of the community now forces regular payment of rent for the areas not purchased and judged to be protected as historical heritage. The agreement also stipulates the compulsive adherence to the state's rental and eviction laws, thus allowing some stubborn residents to remain even though they've violated Christiania's ground rules for staying in the community, yet haven't overstepped Danish law.

"The battle for Christiania's autonomy is no longer in the streets," muses Jørgen, "but in the courtrooms. If we break the agreement with Copenhagen, the city can just threaten to take us to court and win by that alone."

As mentioned by Jørgen and Marie, decisions in Christiania are meant to be taken in the local areas and among the people concerned directly.

There is no voting system per se; consensus is expected to be achieved in order to reach agreement. This is not always the case, though, and controversial subjects such as the ever-recurrent problem of the cannabis trade are the focus of both local neighborhood/area groups and the grand assembly of Christiania. Widely different opinions exist depending on the topic, and conflicts and limited hostilities take place like in any other community.

The grand assembly is convened when the need for it arises and generally brings together several hundred people depending on the issue to be deliberated. Typically an assembly is called to discuss issues addressing the direct future of Christiania and matters of security, such as when shootings occur between weed dealers, police engage in particularly violent incursions, or residents want to make changes to Christiania's constitution. Often assemblies have led to a period of inner reflection where the town has physically sealed itself off from the outside world with barricades and signs for visitors to come back another day.

A time when this was manifested clearly was in the 2007 negotiations between the state and the community of Christiania regarding the decision to agree to or refuse the introduction of certain regulations on housing and the free town itself. Several grand assemblies with hundreds of participants debated the very future of the community and their lives within it. The built-in idealistic principles of reaching mutual consensus were fundamentally challenged during this time of major upheaval. At these meetings, a "conductor" was chosen to direct who could speak next and make sure everyone got a chance to do so, but also to facilitate a common "feeling the air of the room" so as to then propose a decision from what they had heard. This was difficult due to the often-polarized opinions within the deliberations. At the same time, the sense of community that people felt toward each other made them "want it to work," and so people were more open to struggling through the debate and collective decision-making process than, say, someone living in the surrounding city.

A complete consensus with agreement from everyone in the community is a rare thing. Despite all the meetings being announced in the *Weekly Mirror*, which is printed and distributed in Christiania, not all inhabitants choose to participate in the grand assemblies. This might be because of disillusionment with the system, personal disagreements, a lack of time to actively engage in the assembly, or a trust in other community members to make good decisions.

Although in theory everyone is equal within the decision-making processes, as always, certain hierarchies exist. While some people have the time and will to spend hours arguing and working within Christiania's system, others are less skilled at public speaking or political maneuvering, or simply lack the enthusiasm to do so. Others may claim seniority to further their arguments, such as being older or having lived in Christiania longer than others, or are merely resistant to changes and so try to stall them.

"Consensus has two sides to it. First, it gives everyone ownership and a possibility for influence, but it is also frequently messy and requires a lot of patience," Elin explains. "In some cases, like in small gatherings or within groups working closely together on a daily basis, it works really well and major disagreements are rare. On a bigger scale, however, and between groups such as workplaces or in major conflicts, it can be really difficult. Consensus on a large scale such as the grand assemblies with hundreds of people is hard work, and requires time and energy. Oftentimes not everyone has the surplus energy to do this, and some people end up speaking or deciding more than others. Consensus and autonomy teaches you things about yourself, not least of which is to make room for others and realize that sometimes things don't go your way. You learn to accept that, and more often than not you manage to influence things a bit, and generally a better decision is reached by and for everyone."

Elin adds that "when a consensus can't be reached, the default is to not take any decision but instead establish a committee of people from conflicting arguments or proposals to come up with a decision on which they can agree, and then bring it up again before the relevant assembly. Of course it isn't alway fun and games, but no matter how it works out, I find that it is always a way to develop yourself as a person. You learn to take a stand and argue for things that are important to you, but you also learn to compromise and give space."

A shared sentiment among all the people interviewed for this piece was the sense of community and reflection experienced in periods when Christiania was closed to the outside world and thousands of guests streaming through each day: it created room for the strengthening of communal ties. This strategy of taking time to discuss the values and future strategies of autonomy is connected to similar communities elsewhere, such as the Zapatistas, with whom many in Christiania profess a kinship.

As Jørgen noted, "We have had discussions with many communities like ours, and throughout the years we have analyzed the best ways to make consensus-based decisions work. Basically it comes down to two things: empathy with each other, and a willingness to compromise and understand each other's position."

Degrowth, Collective Ownership, and Counterculture

A topic that concerns many autonomous communities and utopian ideals such as those practiced in Christiania is the limits of these ideas, not to mention their survivability. After forty years of struggle and growth, Christiania has reached the physical limits of its area as well as a cap on its population size. Combined with the agreement signed with the Danish state and adoption of a form of property ownership (albeit collective), the danger of stagnation or reversal to private ownership is ever present.

Moving into Christiania is different from relocating to another neighborhood. Due to the restricted amount of space, a limit of around eight hundred residents is placed on the community. Someone has to move out for another person to move in, unless one is born to parents already living in the free town. All members of the local area have a say in who can move in and have veto rights. People applying for a position in a collective or as a resident of a house must meet fellow Christianites and form relationships—something that usually doesn't happen in other Copenhagen neighborhoods. Living in Christiania as a resident also gives one responsibilities to actively participate in decisions both local and spanning the entire free town, such as the discussion about private ownership. This proved to be all too real when a minority of Christianites proposed the possibility of private property in relation to certain houses and apartments. In late 2010, a consensus in the general assembly could not be reached, though, and so every Christianite still pays rent for their home, and doesn't need to put down a deposit on moving in nor do they get any money back on moving out.

One remarkably successful initiative to counter the controversial subject of private ownership (and finance the purchase of the whole area) was the creation of the Christiania share in 2011. Sold as a signed and stamped document, the shares (which are still sold today) attest that the bearer of the document has purchased a part of Christiania. Totaling more than twelve million crowns, not only did the shares help fund the survival of the free town, but they generated thousands of crowns from symbolic co-owners who don't reside in Christiania.

154

NIELSEN

By buying a share, you're not given land or the ability to resell the share for profit. Instead, you buy the certainty that the free town will survive as a place open to anyone and help expand the sense of community to encompass not just the residents but people across the world too.

This practice of highlighting a global sense of community is part of the concept called degrowth. The community, along with others like it, aims to foster a counterculture that opposes and undermines the logic of capitalist accumulation and national boundaries. In Christiania, it is possible to live on a minimal amount of money, oftentimes doing the things that interest the residents and with a transparent view of how it directly benefits the community in which people live. Many Christianites work only part time, and are able to dedicate their time to art, family, and generally just slowing down and living.

The Cuckoo in the Utopian Nest

Despite attracting the majority of the negative media attention directed at Christiania, Pusher Street is crucial to the free town. As Elin underscored, a certain symbiosis exists, with the cannabis trade bringing in buyers who then spend time and money in Christiania, and Christiania's other businesses and venues giving potential customers to the dealers. Still, the relationship has also been unhealthy and damaging at times to the free city.

"In 2015, the police confiscated more than 116 million in cash and cannabis from Christiania alone. We bought these grounds for 115 million, and the police raids haven't even made a dent in the dealers' business," Elin explains. "No wonder the state and city don't agree to concessions with us, given that they think we've got that much money. No one will believe or realize, however, that the free town sees none of the dealers' money, nor would we accept it. It was because of the growing presence of Pusher Street that we lost the original agreement that we had with the state, leading to us as a community having to buy up the area in order to secure our existence. This has come at a price, and Pusher Street continues to be a stone in our shoe."

Despite cannabis being sold openly, it is still illegal, so further concessions to Christiania from the state of Denmark and city of Copenhagen have ground to a halt. "We won't get one more inch of land to build on, or permission to alter or expand our community, as long as the state can point to Pusher Street as a problem," says Ole.

This is in many ways the core problem facing Christiania today. Physically the area in which the community is located has been filled out completely, and it's the state's policy to deny any new expansion or significant alterations to the buildings, which are deemed protected under national heritage regulations, as long as the cannabis trade is ongoing. One might wonder why Christiania does not simply shut down Pusher Street. But such a decision would never be agreed on by consensus because it would violate the basic value of univeral tolerance on which the community is built.

"As things are today," remarks Ole, "Christiania has split into two different factions, each with its own life philosophy and way of operating. One is the consensus-based model of allowing everyone influence as well as free rein to live and do as they will without harming others or violating the constitution of Christiania. The other faction, being the pushers, operates under what is called 'Omerta': the code of honor and silence taken from the Italian mafia. The pushers are uncompromisingly loyal first and foremost to each other, and then Christiania second. Under these conditions, the consensus model can't operate in an effective way, and will always fail if it goes against the interests of the pushers or those people who believe that they should be allowed to stay."

Selling Out or Self-Preservation?

It would be easy to view Christiania as a society in decline, and in some ways this is true. Concessions on the community's autonomy have been made to the state, and the losses will most likely never be recovered. State police now regularly patrol the streets of Christiania. The free city has now become the training ground for the Copenhagen police academy, which sends its young cadets to be hardened by the hostile slurs and feelings they get on entering an enemy territory as well as learn how to deal with bottles, stones, and anger thrown their way when they make an arrest. In turn, this means that many dealers' and residents' experiences with the state now boil down to moments of violent outbursts by the police. And as mentioned earlier, Christiania has to pay rent to the city of Copenhagen for some areas not bought from the state, and is required to obey Danish laws related to property management, housing rentals, and a host of other regulations, thereby taking up much time, energy, and money that could be spent better elsewhere.

Then too, the purchase of the area has led many to become more lax, now functioning more as business owners and groundskeepers, given that their home and community are secure from total eviction. No longer does Christiania actively work to export its philosophy or launch open attacks on capitalism, such as when the radical theater collective Solvognen engaged in spectacular actions in the 1970s. In one famous example, it organized the Santa Claus Army, which saw dozens of people dressed as Santa invade shopping centers to hand out wares to customers free of charge. A widely circulated photo showed one Santa Claus being beaten by the police for being too generous. Solvognen also organized a mass action at Rebild bakker (an area designated as a friendship zone between Denmark and the United States on July 4, 1976) in which hundreds of activists dressed up as the original peoples of the Americas and Greenland (a former Danish colony) to protest the war in Vietnam as well as Danish and US genocides of indigenous communities. Many of these activists tucked sacks of animal blood inside their clothes, which when hit by the police batons that day, sent splashes of red across the ground to symbolize the victims of war, and the action was filmed and broadcast live to thousands of people. The Solvognen Collective continued to organize together for several years afterward and is one of Christiania's most well-known groups.

Christiania has in part survived due to its own efforts at preserving itself as a sustainable and alternative community while balancing regular contact with the surrounding city and Danish state. Some might interpret this and the continued encroachment of state power on the area as selling out to survive, or see such compromises as inevitable, given that Christiania is situated in the heart of a metropolis, and its survival is as much due to the tolerance of the social democratic welfare model as on its skills, coupled with widespread support throughout Denmark.

The ongoing expansion and development is by no means irreversible, and is closely tied in with the potential future legalization of cannabis, making obsolete the criminal elements embedded in Christiania. Similarly, a change might occur in the way in which consensus is practiced within Christiania, allowing the community to solve the stalemate created by Pusher Street and those who wish to preserve the open sale of cannabis. Only time will tell.

That said, Christiania still represents one of the longest-enduring and most successful autonomous communities in western Europe, and continues to offer a unique way of living. As already covered, Christiania's strong institutions created to replace those of the outside society have been key to its survival in overcoming the vacuum that often occurs between breaking with capitalist society and establishing self-governing structures. Though one can live without collective kindergartens, self-managing supply depots, and community-employed groundskeepers, one's quality of life would be far less, so if only for these elements, Christiania should be seen as a place of inspiration, both in terms of its successes and failures.

In Ole's words, "I have been doing this full time for the past forty years, and have been present at almost all the negotiations with the state and been part of most of the major projects. I have worked as an archivist, hairdresser, bartender, and cook, done speaking tours, created exhibitions, and at times been a media spokesperson. Here, I have lived the life I had hoped to live, where I could switch between all kinds of things. Now I am seventy-two, and the archive will be my last big project—to secure our history and legacy."

As Ole adds with pride, "What we have done here is to take an area that was abandoned by the military with almost no functioning infrastructure and completely renovate it. There was no running water, power, or functioning toilets. Structurally, Christiania still works well. If we hadn't been here, this area would have been just another gray and boring part of Copenhagen. We have managed to preserve a completely unique area and history in Copenhagen in pristine condition, and we have carried out the most gentle city renewal possible. Ninety percent of the historic buildings that we took over are still here and in good condition. We have a unique way of living and managing our own affairs, and above all, we have managed to do it under almost impossible conditions."

*

Asbjørn Nielsen is an organizer and journalist based in Copenhagen, currently active with the media platform *Konfront* and the autonomous social center Ungdomshuset. This piece was made possible due to the generosity of the interviewees, helpful feedback from comrades, and lastly, Cindy Milstein, who gave me the opportunity to explore and examine what was right before my nose.

The Bonfires of Autonomy in Cherán

Scott Campbell

For three years, fear ruled San Francisco Cherán, an indigenous P'urhépecha municipality of around twenty thousand people in the Mexican state of Michoacán. During that time, from 2008 to 2011, armed loggers linked to organized crime cartels devastated the municipality's communally held forest. With the collaboration of the police and local government, widely despised and viewed as illegitimate by the populace, the loggers pillaged almost fifty thousand acres of forest, often setting fire to them after removing the trees. Starting at 3:00 a.m., as many as two hundred trucks per day, laden with stolen wood, drove through the community in a display of impunity, and as a continuous reminder of the decimation being inflicted on Cherán's ecosystem and territory. Along with this destruction came murders, disappearances, extortion, and intimidation at the hands of the cartels. Yunuen Torres Ascencio reflects that her "community began to feel the horror caused by vulnerability. As inhabitants of Cherán, we didn't feel safe on the streets, even less so if we were women. It was a systematic assault on the various spheres of community life, reaffirmed by seeing the loggers moving freely through our space, armed and acting like they owned the streets."[1]

Cherán during this time was not unlike many other communities in

---

1. All direct quotations from Yunuen come from interviews conducted between February and May 2019, or the following text: Yunuen Torres Ascencio, "Cherán K'eri o El Gran Cherán: Defender el territorio es defender la vida que lo habita," in *Puntos de cultura viva comunitaria iberoamericana: experiencias compartidas*, ed. Guillermo Cardona Marín and Herman Montoya (Medellín: Sílaba Editores, 2018), 49–63.

Mexico and in particular Michoacán. Then president Felipe Calderón's ostensible "drug war" was raging with calamitous ineffectiveness. His rule from 2006 to 2012 was marked by at least 121,000 murders and 26,000 disappearances. The cartels splintered, asserting themselves into new markets and adopting increasingly brutal tactics. Throughout the various tiers of the state apparatus, fluid and ever-shifting alliances were made between officials and differing cartels. At the local level, such as in Cherán, authorities either colluded or capitulated in the face of organized crime's power. The end result for many Mexicans was horror and helplessness amid the rapidly escalating and exceedingly cruel violence, along with an elevated sense of being abandoned by those who called themselves authorities and claimed all this bloodshed was in the name of security.

Such was the scenario when before dawn on April 15, 2011, the bells of El Calvario Chapel in Cherán rang out in a rhythm distinct from the typical call to Mass. As members of the community gathered, they saw they'd been summoned by a small group of women that had decided to take action. Days earlier, the women witnessed the loggers beginning to cut near La Cofradía, the spring that supplies Cherán's water. That was the breaking point, and on this Friday at 6:00 a.m., the women, armed with nothing more than sticks and Molotov cocktails, blocked one of the logging trucks as it passed by the road in front of the church, unleashing an unforeseen but remarkable series of events.

As the confrontation unfolded, fireworks were set off, alerting the community to an emergency. The women stopped the truck, five loggers were detained and held in the church, and the truck was set on fire. Throughout the morning, more people arrived at El Calvario as the youths of Cherán traversed the community, shouting, as Yunuen recalls, "Come out! We are us. We are Cherán. There's no reason to be afraid! We have to set up our bonfires and secure the town! We have to defend Cherán!" A few hours later, an armed group backed by the municipal police arrived at El Calvario in an attempt to free the five loggers. Clashes erupted, and the police and armed cartel members were forced to retreat empty-handed. That night, a bonfire was lit outside El Calvario.

Fearing an attack by state and/or cartel forces, the next day people erected barricades and checkpoints at each of the five entrances to the community. A volunteer community patrol was organized, and that evening 180 bonfires were lit—one on every block in Cherán's urban center—around which people gathered, stayed vigilant, and discussed what to do next. Having reclaimed control of Cherán from the police, government, and cartels, the first community assembly was held on April 17 to talk about what to do with the detainees and how to move forward. Openly rejecting the return of political parties, the residents decided to create a General Coordinator Commission made up of an equal number of members from each of the four neighborhoods to help meet immediate needs and dialogue with the state. In the weeks that followed, the assembly created fourteen other commissions to address specific facets of community life.[2] All the commissions were guided by principles agreed on in the community assembly, such as "equal representation from the four neighborhoods, that its members were elected in assemblies, and that the work they did was voluntary or on behalf of the community without receiving economic renumeration in return."[3]

---

2. The commissions created were the following: Honor and Justice, Bonfires, Press and Propaganda, Food, Finance, Education and Culture, Forest, Water, Sanitation, Youth, Agriculture and Livestock, Commerce, Identity, and Health.

3. Orlando Aragón Andrade, "Otra democracia es posible. Aprendizajes para una democracia radical en México desde la experiencia política de Cherán," in *Demodiversidad. Imaginar nuevas posibilidades democráticas*, ed. Boaventura de Sousa Santos and José Manuel Mendes (Mexico City: Akal, 2017), 475–99.

At the time, the community assembly's decisions were made in light of a relatively spontaneous uprising that succeeded in immediately dismantling the corrupt and hierarchical local power structure. The predominant concerns were preparing for a potential counterattack, preventing a return to what had just been overthrown, and meeting the needs of the twenty thousand inhabitants. The political or ideological orientations of the nascent movement were primarily expressed in the form that the decision-making process took, an agreement not to allow the return of political parties, and the slogan/demand/aspiration that's in use to this day: "For the security, justice, and reconstitution of our territory." Yet through these prescient early decisions and way in which they were made, Cherán was also laying the foundation for what's still in place: an autonomous communal government, in which power resides in the hands of an organized municipality.

The Structure and Function
of the Communal Government

In the months following the uprising, Cherán largely existed in a state of self-imposed siege as it sought to secure itself and consolidate the victory it had won. The General Coordinator Commission held negotiations with the state and federal governments, primarily concerning protection from cartel retribution. Such concerns were very real, as during the first year following the uprising at least six community members from Cherán were killed in cartel attacks. At the same time, social movements from around Mexico mobilized in solidarity with Cherán, and organized caravans to bring aid and supplies to the community.

Statewide elections were scheduled for November 13, 2011. In June, the community assembly resolved that it would not allow the state to install voting booths in Cherán. Weeks later, Cherán officially requested that it be allowed to choose its own municipal government through *usos y costumbres*.[4] The Michoacán Electoral Institute denied the request, but in October 2011, the community moved forward with the process anyway, replacing the transitional General Coordinator and fourteen other commissions with a more permanent structure. Following legal action taken by the community and movement lawyers, both the federal electoral court and Mexico's Supreme Court later ruled that Cherán had the right to select its government by usos y costumbres.

Nombramientos and the Assemblies

"Elections" is not a word used inside Cherán to describe its way of choosing the members of its government. The process is instead called a nombramiento, meaning a "naming" or "appointment." Though a notable occurrence, the nombramiento is not a one-off event as elections are viewed in most of the world. Nor is it the peak expression of Cherán's autonomous communal government. Rather, it is one function within an ongoing process, best understood as the renewal or transition point of a dynamic system that consistently remains in operation as a result of active community participation during the span between each nombramiento.

For all its rhetoric to the contrary, the coercive and hierarchical govern-

---

4. Literally "uses and customs," this is a general term used to refer to indigenous forms of governance. Under Mexican and international law, indigenous communities technically have the right to choose their local authorities via usos y costumbres, usually in a form of community assembly. This method should not by default be conflated with autonomous governance, as in many communities where it is practiced, political parties and the state have successfully co-opted it.

ment of the modern nation-state is most often experienced by its subjects as something distinct from them, an apparatus largely operating under the power of its own oppressive inertia, with "democracy" the act of choosing among undesirable options every few years. Leaders and parties are elected, and subsequently dedicate their terms to consolidating power in preparation for the next election. As such, adding "communal" in front of "government" as well as speaking of "members of the government" may fail in conveying the shift within Cherán since 2011. These crucial distinctions become clearer by walking through the nombramiento, which requires walking through the communal government structure of bonfires, assemblies, and councils, which in turn requires walking through the structure of the community, contextualized by the physical and social infrastructure created during the rebellion.

As noted above, bonfires were established on every block in Cherán during the uprising. Burning nightly, they were the primary point of encounter for residents in the initial months of the movement. Each bonfire is numbered, and what block people live on determines their specific bonfire membership. While most of the physical bonfires are no longer present, they remain as organizational structures. Each has a rotating coordinator who facilitates the regular meetings of bonfire members. This is the first level of organization of the communal government, where residents can raise concerns or make proposals among their neighbors. Every three years, when the nombramiento occurs (so far in 2011, 2015, and 2018), members of each bonfire gather to discuss if any of their participants would be good nominees for the various government councils. These are the Council of Elders (Concejo Mayor), the Communal Treasury (Tesorería Comunal), and eight specialized councils. It is deeply frowned on to nominate oneself. Instead, members suggest other members of their bonfire. If there is consensus about a nominee, and a willingness and ability on their part to serve, this is documented and brought to the neighborhood assembly.

Cherán is comprised of four neighborhoods—a structure that has been in place since its establishment. The neighborhoods are referred to in Spanish as the first, second, third, and fourth, or by their names in P'urhépecha: Jarhúkutini, Kétsikua, Karhákua, and Parhíkutini, respectively.[5] All the bonfires of each neighborhood meet jointly in a neighborhood assembly. Neighborhood assemblies meet weekly at a regular date, time, and location. Reminders about neighborhood assemblies are made through speakers mounted in each neighborhood and by the community radio station, Radio Fogata. In cases of emergency, a neighborhood assembly can be called by residents of the neighborhood or the communal government, and the Neighborhood Coordinating Council (Consejo Coordinador de los Barrios) notifies the bonfire coordinators, who then notify bonfire members.

During the nombramiento, the neighborhood assemblies first select the members of the Council of Elders, comprised of twelve people, three from each neighborhood. All councillors must be forty-five years or older, and beginning in 2015, as a result of a proposal approved in all the neighborhood assemblies, at least one from each neighborhood must be a woman. In the assembly, a spokesperson from each bonfire that's nominating someone for the council introduces the nominee and hands over the support documentation. The spokesperson has five minutes to state why the nominee has

---

5. Within Cherán, around fourteen thousand inhabitants reside in these four neighborhoods. There are also two smaller communities (*tenencias*) in the municipality. One, Santa Cruz Tanaco, does not participate in the communal government but instead has its own independent form of organization. The other, El Cerecito, participates in the assemblies of the first neighborhood.

been chosen and would be a good fit. The nominee then has five minutes to accept or reject the nomination, and state their reasons why. After this process has occurred for all nominees, they stand on chairs at the front of the assembly, and everyone else physically lines up in front of the nominee they most support. The number of people in each line is counted off out loud, and the nominees with the three longest lines become the three members of the Council of Elders for that neighborhood. If all three selected are men, the woman with the longest line takes the place of the man who had the third-longest line. At a later assembly, this same process names members of the other councils, with the exception that instead of three, only one person from each neighborhood is chosen for each council. With no campaigning and utilizing infrastructure already in place, Cherán's municipal nombramientos only cost about US$3,300.

After the neighborhood assemblies all choose their members for the Council of Elders, a day of celebration occurs. Energetic marches leave from each neighborhood and meet in the community's central plaza to shouts of "the neighborhoods united will never be defeated!" The new councillors are introduced neighborhood by neighborhood with cheers and confetti. They may address and also receive words from the community. At the 2018 celebration documented by TV Cherán, a community member shared this: "I want to deliver a small message to the new Council of Elders in whom we have placed our trust. Once again, our community is showing and telling all of you through this new process that political parties must not exist here, religions must not exist here. What must exist here is equality. And if we have put our trust in you, it is because we want you to support the well-being of our community and that our forests continue to be respected."

While most matters facing the community can be resolved within the government councils or neighborhood assemblies, there is occasionally the need for a community assembly. This is the highest decision-making body and ultimate authority in Cherán. A community assembly can be called for by the Council of Elders or any neighborhood assembly. Both the community and neighborhood assemblies make decisions via consensus. As these assemblies represent the communal voice of Cherán and decisions made there are seen as collectively held responsibilities, community members are encouraged and expected to use the assembly as the place to bring concerns, doubts, or differences of opinion on the matters at hand. If an issue before the assembly proves difficult to resolve, repeated assemblies may be held until consensus is reached. Yunuen, a former member of the Youth Council, sums up the structure of Cherán's government, noting, "The bonfire represents the base of our organization, the base that proposes what path our community should take. The second space is the neighborhood assembly, where discussions and important matters are openly addressed. The third space is the community assembly, the union and expression of the four neighborhoods of Cherán."

A Circle of Councils

No one part of the government can operate without the consent and participation of the whole—with the whole, in this case, being the community of Cherán. According to the structure of the communal government as determined for 2018–21, the whole is made up of interdependent circles. Starting with the "circumference," the four neighborhoods are linked together in a circle that encompasses the eight Specialized Operating Councils (Consejos Operativos Especializados). The Council of Elders, Communal Treasury, and Main Operating Council (Consejo Operativo Principal) are found within the next "interior" circle. Lastly, at the "center" in a circle by itself is the K'eri Tángurhikua, the community assembly. While the locus of authority is centered in the community assembly, it and all the government councils rest on the foundation of the four neighborhoods joined together.

Each council plays an important part in the communal government and therefore the functioning of the community generally. It's important to re-emphasize that these councils are comprised of residents who've been asked by their community to temporarily serve the interests of Cherán as part of the communal government. They are not technocrats or politicians. Julio Medina Hurtado, an oral surgeon who served on the Social Programs Council, explains, "All of us who were in the government or are there now, we left our family, our work, our free time, in order to serve the community. … I didn't know what I was facing, what kind of work I was going to be doing. Obviously, no one has the experience because it's different work than what we do day in and day out. Yet we all have the ability to do it."[6]

With decision-making powers resting firmly in the hands of the assemblies, the councils serve as administrative nodes to implement the policies determined by the assemblies. For example, the duties of the Council of Elders include ensuring the proper functioning of the other councils, being the face of the community in front of the state and federal governments, creating a communal development plan for its term in government that is then presented for approval to the community assembly, auditing the municipal treasury, and bringing pertinent matters to the assemblies so that decisions can be made.

6. All direct quotations from Julio come from an interview conducted on April 7, 2019.

Additionally, there is a qualitative aspect to its administrative role. The members of the Council of Elders are expected to be the moral authorities of the community. The assumption is that in completing their tasks, the councillors will be guided by and adhere to the values of the community along with the communal structures that placed them in their positions. For their three-year term, they will be the caretakers of what was born of sacrifice and struggle in 2011, and above all are expected to use wisdom and humility to see that the community continues to grow along the right path for those who come after. By doing so, they can reciprocate the trust, honor, and respect placed in them by their fellow community members.

Within the same circle as the Council of Elders is the Communal Treasury. It manages local income as well as funds obtained from the state and federal governments, and oversees budgets for the community and each council, with oversight in turn from the Council of Elders and community assembly. Completing this circle is the Main Operating Council, a gathering of all thirty-two members of the eight specialized councils. Alongside the treasury and Council of Elders, the Main Operating Council coordinates the work of the eight specialized councils and contributes to the Council of Elders' creation of the communal development plan.

During the first communal government, from 2011 to 2015, there were six Specialized Operating Councils, which are still ongoing and fill the following roles.

The Local Administration Council (Consejo de Administración Local) is tasked with public works, lighting, gardening, and maintaining the sports fields and main plaza. It also collects garbage under a "zero-waste" program. This council operates three garbage trucks, which collect trash, recyclables, and organic waste. The trash is taken to the council-run landfill, the recyclables are sold, and the organic material is turned into compost for community agricultural projects. The council administers a water purification project too. On the top of Kukundikata Hill, the communal government constructed a rain-capture system believed to be the largest in Latin America. This system not only guarantees an emergency water supply; the council also purifies this water and makes it available to the community at a low cost, with a twenty-liter bottle costing eight pesos (around forty cents in US dollars).

The Civic Affairs Council (Consejo de Asuntos Civiles) administers educational, public health, cultural, and sports programs. Cherán has thirty-one schools, and a major focus is the construction of an educational system reflective of the community. As Heriberto Ramos, a high school principal, explains, "We have two important projects: one, to continue rescuing and recovering our language, and the other, to not imitate the curriculums of outsiders that have come in and created individualist mentalities."[7] To augment that effort, the council runs a House of Culture, which hosts music, art, dance, and P'urhépecha language workshops as well as a children's orchestra. Cherán has two health clinics and a small hospital, along with private doctors' offices. In the field of public health, the council administers vaccination campaigns, mosquito eradication efforts, and health awareness campaigns.

The Council for the Procurement, Security, and Mediation of Justice (Consejo de Procuración, Vigilancia y Mediación de Justicia) is more often referred to as the Honor and Justice Council. When the municipal police

---

7. Heriberto Ramos, "Participación de maestros de la comunidad," in *Cherán K'eri. 5 años de autonomía*, ed. Fernanda Martínez, Yunuen Torres, Meriene Betancourt, René Olvera, and Alberto Colin (Cherán: En cortito que's pa'largo, 2017), 85–88.

were run out of town, their weapons and vehicles were used to create Community Patrol (Ronda Comunitaria) and Forest Protection (Guarda-bosques) formations. Those are overseen by this council, and their memberships are rotating and determined by the neighborhood assemblies. The Community Patrol, made up of a hundred people, maintains checkpoints at the entrances to Cherán, and responds to concerns reported to it by the bonfires and assemblies, while the Forest Protection units ensure that the loggers do not return. Individuals of all genders participate in these groups. Neither group is viewed as a law enforcement formation, but rather as organized members of the community, selected and held accountable by the community, working to maintain the security reclaimed by the 2011 uprising. Instead of detecting, preventing, or punishing "crime" within a legalistic framework, the council concerns itself with "anticommunal conduct," in which case the Community Patrol may intervene. Depending on the incident, such cases may be resolved by mediation, repayment for damages, community service, or referral for rehabilitation or psychological treatment. If the implicated individual refuses to cooperate, they may be placed for a short time in a *kataperakua*, which translates roughly as "where we all may fall into." It is an open-air, roofless cell where the individual must endure the elements and reflect on their behavior. It is utilized about twice a month, often as the result of fights. In the rare event of a serious incident, a decision may be made by the council to refer the matter to the Michoacán state prosecutor. To date, five homicide cases have been referred to the state. The council also oversees traffic control, responses to fires or other emergencies, and civil matters such as disputes over contracts or debts.

As mentioned above, Cherán does receive funding from the state and federal governments. Much of this comes in the form of social assistance programs. Implementation of these programs falls to the Social, Economic, and Cultural Programs Council (Consejo de los Programas So-ciales, Económicos y Culturales). While 96 percent of Cherán's adults are employed, 73 percent of the population is classified by the Mexican government as living in poverty. Cherán's largest source of income is from remittances sent by the more than ten thousand of its residents who have migrated, primarily to the United States. Given the economic conditions inherited by the 2011 movement, the community has agreed in assembly to continue receiving assistance. These programs include food staples for the elderly, stores offering subsidized food and milk, housing support, temporary employment programs, life insurance for single mothers, and pension programs. Asked about the dynamic of working with state agencies, Julio, a former council member, says, "They had their way of doing things and they wanted us to do it their way. But we had to prioritize our form of organization. I would tell them, 'You're going to give us this resource and you want us to show how it was used, of course. But the way in which that resource is delivered depends on us, and we want you to be respectful of our way of internal organizing.' And they told us, 'That's fine, do it.'"

The Neighborhood Coordinating Council serves as the link between the neighborhood assemblies and the rest of the communal government. It monitors and assists in the convening of neighborhood assemblies, and communicates their decisions to the communal government. Additionally, it organizes *faenas* (voluntary collective workdays) in each neighborhood. Along with these internal activities, it facilitates visits from outside organizations and collectives plus has a mobilizing role, organizing Cherán's solidarity actions. A 2017 government report noted its hosting of an indigenous communities gathering in Cherán, a march and takeover of Pemex gasoline facilities in response to neoliberal energy reform policies, gathering supplies for teachers and protesting alongside them against neoliberal educational reforms, and collecting supplies for the autonomous community of Santa María Ostula.[8]

The municipality of Cherán has about sixty-seven thousand acres of communally held land. The administration of this land falls to the Communal Properties Council (Consejo de los Bienes Comunales), which carries out work along two main lines. One line is the reforestation of the logged forest, which includes replanting trees, soil remediation, and creating firebreaks and patrol routes. More than twenty-four hundred acres have been reforested since 2011. The council also administers the community's businesses. These include a nursery, which grows plants for the reforesting effort along with selling additional trees to Mexico's National Forest Commission and the public. There is also a sawmill that only uses dead or sustainably harvested wood to produce lumber to sell as well as for building needed infrastructure in the community. Finally, there is a construction materials business, offering low-cost, prefabricated materials to community residents. These businesses not only produce income and employment for the community; what is produced is intended to meet the community's needs. Who works in each of these businesses is decided by the neighborhood assemblies, while pay is determined by the council.

Starting with the second communal government in 2015, two new councils were added to the original six: the Youth Council (Consejo de los Jóvenes) and Women's Council (Consejo de la Mujer). María de la Luz Torres Tomás, a former member of the Women's Council, describes how her council came about. "The need for representation of women in the community came up in the bonfires, as women are the foundation of the

---

8. Gobierno Comunal, *Segundo informe de gobierno comunal 2015–2018* (Cherán: Gobierno Comunal, 2017), 58–59.

family and the 2011 uprising."[9] Yunuen, a former Youth Council member, remarks that "as the women were recognized as initiators of the uprising, it was the youths who supported their efforts, and later the rest of the community came along. In planning the structure of the second communal government in 2015, the proposal [for a Youth Council] was brought forward by the grandparents, the elders of the community. Discussion regarding the creation of Youth and Women's Councils took place in every assembly, and they were both approved."

The Youth Council focuses primarily on creating youth spaces that promote culture, art, recreation, sports, and employment, and prevent addiction and alcoholism. For the first three weeks of the uprising, the schools were shut down. During that time, the youths stepped up to organize activities for the community's children. Drawing on this experience, today the council organizes workshops in all the schools covering a variety of topics: literature, rap, video, photography, radio, storytelling, the P'urhépecha language, and the history of the movement. It also hosts film screenings, mural projects, reforestation efforts, concerts, and cultural festivals geared toward children and young people. Members of the council facilitate visits from outside groups, and are often tapped to travel to represent Cherán at national and international gatherings, conferences, and events. As Yunuen underscores, "All the activities we carry out always remember the movement. Everything is directed toward conveying and strengthening the sense of the movement, and ensuring its continuation."

Though not projects of the Youth Council, it coordinates links and trainings with three youth-run media projects in Cherán. One is Radio Fogata,

---

9. All direct quotations from María de la Luz come from an interview conducted in February 2019.

a community radio station started in August 2011 when solidarity organizations smuggled a transmitter into the community. The second is TV Cherán, which began in 2014 and airs on a local station, though only sporadically as it has been a difficult project to maintain. And finally, there is Fogata Kejtsitani, meaning Fire of Living Memory, an oral history project that organizes forums, publications, and multimedia projects oriented around the journey of Cherán since the uprising. All these projects operate according to their own assemblies, and have guidelines determining participation and content.[10]

As outlined in the 2017 government report, the Women's Council defines its objective as "impacting the quality of life for the women of Cherán and their families. To reduce inequality, gender-based violence, sex discrimination, and for full integration into the community." To that end, the council administers a variety of programs. It holds talks on women's rights as well as gatherings to discuss and further the role of women in the community. Workshops are also held on healthy and hygienic food preparation, including in the schools and restaurants. Together with the Community Patrol, the council makes rounds to check on community members' health—in particular the elderly—and facilitates medical checkups, dental work, and transportation to hospitals outside the community as needed. It also organizes events to raise awareness about mental health and addiction, and uses some of its funding to provide wheelchairs, walkers, canes, and other materials to residents who have a need but cannot afford them on their own. Of the council's work, María de la Luz says she is most proud of a project initiated in 2018 called the Women's House, aiming "to recover

---

10. For Radio Fogata, see http://radiofogata.org/. For TV Cherán, see https://is
.gd/TVCheran. For Fogata Kejtsitani, see https://kejtsitani.wordpress.com/.

the wisdom of the grandmothers and work with traditional medicine. We have an organic garden and soon will form a women's cooperative."

Considering the numerous responsibilities and projects of councils, it is clearly more than the four members of each council can carry out on their own. To that end, each council may create commissions to assist in the completion of their tasks. These commissions must be approved by the neighborhood assemblies, and their members are also chosen by the assemblies. Overall, around three hundred people hold some type of position in the communal government. Everyone is paid for their service, with salaries determined by the community assembly. A government post is not a lucrative position, though, with most earning far less than the jobs they put on hold in order to enter the government. For example, members of the Council of Elders receive 8,000 pesos (about US$425) per month, making them by far the lowest-paid government officials in the state of Michoacán. Before the uprising, Cherán's municipal officials on average received 32,000 pesos per month (about US$1,700).[11]

Members of the councils act as representatives for the neighborhood that chose them too. If a resident has a concern, complaint, or proposal, along with bringing it to the bonfire or neighborhood assembly, they may approach the appropriate council. The council is expected to work with the individual until the matter is satisfactorily resolved. The council offices

---

11. Details on salaries can be found in Patricia Monreal, "En Michoacán, ayuntamientos pobres con funcionarios bien pagados," *Revolución 3.0*, May 31, 2016, http://michoacantrespuntocero.com/en-michoacan-ayuntamientos-pobres-con-funcionarios-bien-pagados/; Rodrigo J. Pinto-Escamilla, "La Parangua. Institución instituyente en la autonomía de Cherán" (master's thesis, Instituto Tecnológico y de Estudios Superiores de Occidente, 2016), 21–22.

are housed in the Communal House, formerly known as the Municipal Palace, the seat of the former government until it was taken over during the uprising.

All council decisions are made by consensus. Julio explains how this worked on the Social Programs Council: "When we had to make a decision, we discussed it among the four of us. Each person offered their opinion. After each person gave their opinion, we said, 'You know what, we believe the most important thing is that we're all working on the same side.' From the mix of ideas, together we drew out one that was the best. We didn't say, 'Who votes for this and who votes for that?' No, no, no. We made ourselves aware of others' positions and reflected on our own position with that awareness. We never had an argument or problem in making decisions."

While each iteration of the communal government lasts three years, with a prohibition on reelection, a member may be removed from their position at any time. Since 2011, this has happened on several occasions. Generally, this is a result of an individual failing to fulfill the duties of their position. When that occurs, the person in question receives a "warning" from the neighborhood assembly that named them to their post. If after three "warnings" the problem has not been resolved, the assembly thanks them for their service and notifies them that they have been removed from their position.

Through the bonfires and assemblies to the various councils, Cherán's communal government emerged, functions, and continues to exist as a result of the community's impulse. As opposed to something apart, it is an integral expression of a people collectively administering their lives, determining and addressing their needs, and defending their territory. It is a government that has a clear structure, allowing it to complete concrete tasks, yet also an organicity, fluidity, and accountability as a result of being given shape by the community, and being consistently overseen and directed by it. Whether it be through the bonfires, assemblies, or councils, there are multiple points of access into the government for individuals or groups to express concerns, bring proposals, and impact the trajectory of the communal government project. In return, these various formations that give shape to the government hold the expectation and hope that this is precisely what members of the community will do. It is a reciprocity founded on the vision of a government as being of the community and equally the community being of the government.

The Social and Political Foundations

While both its structure and logistics are impressive, the question remains, Why did the communal government take this shape? When several women stepped in front of a logging truck on April 15, 2011, it was an act of defiant desperation, not a tactic in the service of a larger political program. Yet as the uprising swept oppressive forces, such as the cartels, police, and municipal authorities, from the territory of Cherán, an opening was created that could have been filled in a variety of ways. Into the vacuum stepped the power of an organized community transitioning almost seamlessly from revolt to a process of consolidation that led to the creation of the communal government that's still in place. The social and political factors that facilitated that process are the same ones that inform, are expressed in, and are further enriched through Cherán's communal government. Broadly, these factors can be understood as the active organization of the community before 2011, the experience of political parties in Cherán, and the intersections of collectively expressed identity, connection to territory, and understanding of being in community.

Until 1988, there was only one political party in Cherán, the Institutional Revolutionary Party (PRI). During this time, the community also used the practice of neighborhood assemblies to elect by consensus its municipal authorities, who would serve in the PRI's name. While assemblies were used, the government structure was nothing like what exists today. Rather, it was the typical hierarchical model of a municipal president (or mayor) and various department heads. Similarly, before the imposition of the municipal police by the state, Cherán organized its own voluntary patrol to safeguard the community.

Another component of community organization before 2011 can be found in the neighborhoods. Yunuen notes that "since its founding, Cherán has been organized by neighborhoods—a system that allowed for the rethinking and activation of our collective ways of completing various communal tasks, be they commissions for festivities or other local responsibilities." While the communal government is secular, Cherán is an overwhelmingly observant Catholic community. Religious festivals, particularly those celebrating its patron saint, Saint Francis, are important events. Each neighborhood holds one, and in order to do so they come together yearly to decide how to organize their festival, raise funds, create commissions to complete the necessary tasks, and choose the leaders of those commissions.

Taken together, when the uprising occurred, Cherán, both in its collective memory and practical organization, had tools at the ready for coming together as a community in the absence of political authority—one they didn't want anyway. A text produced by the oral history project Fogata Kejtsitani affirms that after the uprising, "the only thing that mattered was to defend the community, and by doing so to make it remember, re-create, and resume its own form of government and communal participation that would lead to the construction of municipal autonomy."[12] Yunuen elaborated further, saying, "The moment this framework was created was at the beginning of the uprising in April 2011, when the need to organize ourselves was urgent. In this sense, we just picked up the forms that P'urhépecha communities have historically used. The elders began to mention, 'This is what worked before and this is how it was done.' From there the Community Patrol was resumed, the councils restarted, and that's how the structure of the communal government was built."

Reactivating past systems of community organization also meant rejecting the present structure and ensuring its qualities did not infiltrate the autonomous process that was underway. Above all, this meant the absolute and unequivocal rejection of political parties, and by extension, the electoral and representative systems of which they are an integral part.

The rationale behind this rejection can be found in events that transpired in Cherán starting in 1988, a year of major rupture within the Mexican political system. In the community, the newly emerged Party of the Democratic Revolution (PRD) began contesting elections too. Municipal elections changed from consensus-based assemblies to secret balloting according to party allegiance. As Rodrigo Pinto-Escamilla writes, "The rotation of parties beginning in 1988 divided many people, including neighbors and families. . . . Instead of symbolizing an alternative to the only ruling party, the arrival of the PRD caused community division. Instead of being

---

12. This text, quoted several times in this chapter, is the following: Mario Camarena Ocampo, Rocelia Rojas Guardían, Miriam Daniela Níniz Rojas, and Yunuen Torres Ascencio, "2011 Ueeratini mindakua juramuticheeri Cheranio. Nombramientos del gobierno comunal a partir de 2011 en Cherán," in *Fogata Kejtsitani: Memoria Viva* (2018).

committed to the community, residents became committed to a party."[13] The 2008 election proved exceptionally divisive and inconclusive, and ultimately led to the victory of PRI candidate Roberto Bautista. This was followed by the murders, kidnappings, and disappearances of those who opposed his administration, and the onset of the terror and ecocide perpetrated by his allies, the loggers and cartels.

Rightfully so, elections and political parties are seen as a form of violence in Cherán. The Fogata Kejtsitani text asserts that "the electoral process is a violent matter. What ruled were clientelist relationships with political parties, ending in fierce violence expressed by the political parties and a loss of communal feeling. . . . On April 15, 2011, the people decided 'no more political parties.' The parties only created division among people and only sought the people out when they needed votes, obtaining a benefit for them at a cost to the community. The movement broke with the clientelist bonds of the parties and state government."

So ingrained is the rejection of political parties in Cherán that electoral or political party propaganda is prohibited in the community and confiscated at checkpoints by the Community Patrol, including the removal of political bumper stickers from cars. Visits from outside government officials belonging to any party must be coordinated with the community beforehand. If permitted to enter, they are usually only allowed to do so briefly in order to conduct the necessary work and without the presence of any media. As well, any state or federal employees who work in Cherán must be residents of the community. And Cherán continues to prohibit

---

13. All direct quotations from Rodrigo are from Rodrigo J. Pinto-Escamilla, "La Parangua. Institución instituyente en la autonomía de Cherán" (master's thesis, Instituto Tecnológico y de Estudios Superiores de Occidente, 2016).

the installation of voting booths in its territory for state and federal elections.

In place of a model imposed from outside that only brought division, violence, and ecological devastation to the community, a priority of Cherán's
recuperated system of community administration is the healing of those
wounds through building a sense of community united by identity and
place. This process is aided by the fact that 95 percent of Cherán's residents
are originally from Cherán. The significant consequence of this is that
while over the decades the municipality has passed through varying
periods of stability, division, violence, and uprisings, these phases have all
been experienced as a community and are retained in its collective memory, allowing for a common basis of discussion, reflection, and action.

A glimpse of this commonality can be seen in how residents refer to one
another. As in many other indigenous and ejidal communities throughout
Mexico, members of Cherán call themselves *comuneras/os*. Though it
refers to an individual, the word itself—containing the roots of "common"
and "community"—places the individual within a community context. In
Cherán this is understood as a reciprocal relationship with implications for
the communal government. As the Fogata Kejtsitani document explains,
with the word comunera/o, "We are referring to belonging to the community—when a person recognizes themselves as part of the community and
the community recognizes the person as part of it." In order to participate
in any sphere of the communal government, one must be a comunera/o.[14]

---

14. When asked about how the 5 percent of the people who aren't from Cherán
fit into this framework, Yunuen replies that usually those from the outside who end
up in Cherán do so out of a commitment, often marriage, that makes them part of
the community. After five years, they may be named to a government position.

In Cherán, however, there is an even deeper communally held understanding that links individual with community. An explanation is complicated by the traversing of three languages, two of them rooted in colonization. In English, comunera/o simply becomes "resident," or at best, "community member," losing important qualities in the translation. Yet the same occurs for comunera/o as the closest Spanish approximation of the P'urhépecha word it is being translated from, *ireti*—a word that Cherán's communal government defines as follows, quoting from the Fogata Kejtsitani text:

> The ireti is that comunero to whom corresponds obligations and rights; that as part of the population and originally from this place, is familiar with, adopts, and respects the *juramukatecha*—the norms—as well as the *juramukuecha*—or internal government institutions—accepting the roles and responsibilities that go along with them.
>
> In such a way, the noun *ireti*, singular, and *ireticha*, plural, indicates one who is originally from this place, or those who live and make community.... Participation is premised on the investiture or quality of being a P'urhépecha comunero affiliated with our community of Cherán.

To be a part of Cherán is not an individual choice but rather a communal one. It is also an active process with responsibilities and expectations, yet ones that are borne by individuals together in community. For decades this found expression in neighborhood assemblies and religious festivals, and continues now via the communal government.

Cherán's process of governance is viewed through this lens of integrating individual and community. While usos y costumbres is generally limited to how elections happen, Cherán's Statute of Principles, drafted and approved by the community assembly in 2011, defines it as a "normative internal system that not only regulates the community's government but also social coexistence." Or as the Fogata Kejtsitani document puts it, "At the national level, voting is an individual matter. In the community, it has been turned into a collective decision." Elsewhere the document notes that "the idea of organizing by councils is a way of governing that is concerned with the different needs of the community rather than of the municipal authorities. The operating councils are guided by the sense of taking on their commitments in a communitarian manner, where if someone is in charge of coordinating a project it is not meant to exclude or limit the participation of the community in general. To the contrary, the idea is for the always active participation of comuneros, even if they aren't part of the government structure."

Taken together, the picture that emerges is not of a government that is institutionalized apart from the people or attempts to impose itself on a populace. One instead sees the reverse in Cherán: a community that has institutionalized a government in the service of its collective and communal needs, experiences, and identity. It is the ireticha who gather at bonfires and in assemblies, and assume council positions to guide a collectively bound community forward in autonomy.

It is notable that within residents' descriptions of the guiding forces behind Cherán's government, there is scant mention of constructs such as capitalism, the state, and colonialism. Yet for those looking at or writing about Cherán from the outside, it is not uncommon for the community's struggle to be framed in such terms. While such interpretations are not incorrect, they are more likely to reflect the writing of the outside author's political orientation onto the struggle of Cherán as opposed to locating within the community itself a communal understanding and expression of how its own autonomous project engages with those systems. As such, explicit discussion of these forces has not been a priority within this piece (indeed written by an outsider), as the analysis and framing of Cherán's struggle has attempted to adhere to how the community, through documents and interviews, presents and conceptualizes itself and its process.

Of course, this is not to say that there is no awareness of these factors within the movement, but more that they are ancillary concerns, navigated as they present themselves instance by instance versus in their conceptual totality. Julio of the Social Programs Council portrays it this way: "Basically, we started this struggle to defend ourselves as a community. And as a consequence of this, it put us in rebellion against the different systems of oppression. I think this is a plus for our movement. But above all the essence of it was to eradicate insecurity. We needed a pretext, something to set off the 'ya basta,' and that was the looting of our natural resources, the devastation of the forests. Beyond or after the uprising, it generated this dynamic, this struggle against different systems. I think that one brings about the other."

From the outset and to this day, the uprising in Cherán has always been articulated by what it is *for*, most concisely contained by the aforementioned slogan, "For the security, justice, and reconstitution of our territory." In the service of what the community was for, it rose up and soon after created an autonomous communal government. As Julio points out, being *for something* placed them in opposition to oppressive forces. Yet with the exception of the exclusion of political parties, this did not take the shape of a political line fighting certain systems but instead a configuration and willingness to fight whatever got in the way of their communal aspirations, regardless of the name it took. Yunuen underscores that "in the assemblies and bonfires we understand terms such as 'capitalism,' perhaps in a general way. But we know that in the face of the impossible, what we've built communally confronts all these adversities. The state is always looking for a way to pressure us in one form or another, on occasion conditioning aid or programs that it has to deliver to us just like any other municipality. We're aware of this and have faced it through organizing. We ourselves are changing many concepts, we are reclaiming what is ours, and although the path remains difficult, the forces of Cherán remain firm."

The Experience of Living in Autonomy

Before 2011, the people of Cherán were plagued by violence, division, and environmental destruction. Then one Friday morning, an act of disobedience, whose outcome was uncertain, pierced the mantel of fear that had shrouded the community. In doing so, an opening was created for others to step through in rebellion. It was a rebellion not only against the external factors that had oppressed the residents of Cherán but also a rebellion against the internal conditioning and ways of being that these external factors had coerced them into assuming in order to survive. The fear was not vanquished, yet it lost its power over individuals as they united in collective action to face, hold, and defy that fear together in community. It was together that Cherán was able to dismantle the forces that had subjugated the community and put in their place a model rooted in communality that led to the victory of autonomy.

More than any other site or phenomenon, it was the bonfire that was the primary space for a reencountering of community for the inhabitants of Cherán. As the Fogata Kejtsitani document notes, "The days passed quickly at the bonfires. There was never a moment without a good conversation, a discussion about how to solve the community's problems, how we saw them, how others saw them, how they were seen from the outside.

They were the communication centers and concentration points for ideas, where dialogue flowed between elders and the coming generations. It was around the fire that a way of participating in community was rekindled that built a government represented by and for the comuneros of Cherán."

This experience was occurring daily and nightly, in at least 180 locations simultaneously around Cherán. As Julio describes it, "We've generated a consciousness of *comunalidad*. We have to help ourselves." The repeated coming together, the breaking down of isolation and individualism, and the continued experience of being in community, along with knowing that others are going through the same practice all over the municipality, established firm bonds of commitment and responsibility that would be carried on many shoulders. While speaking specifically about the youths of Cherán, Yunuen movingly elaborates on this idea, commenting, "What Cherán teaches us is 'the *I* has become *us*' as a result of living in community."

There is a further experiential significance to the bonfire. In this piece, the Spanish word *fogata* has been translated as "bonfire." Yet as with co-munera/o above, there is a deeper quality linked to the P'urhépecha word, *parangua*. As Rodrigo explains, "The parangua is the traditional P'urhépecha kitchen that establishes unity; it is set up in such a way to allow for the cohabitation of all members of the house. ... It is a space of encounter, cohesion, expression, and family reflection. Within it, the rhythm of everyday life stops to create a space for the sharing of food, warmth, thoughts, and feelings." With the uprising and bonfires, this intimate family space was shifted from the home onto the streets and spread to include the community as a whole, breaking down differences and extending familial bonds to one's neighbors, who then reciprocated.

Lastly, as with many peoples, fire holds a special significance in P'ur-hépecha culture and is latent with meaning that fed directly into the experience of the lighting of 180 bonfires. "Symbolically, for P'urhépecha communities, the building of the bonfire represents strength," writes Yunuen. "Fire, *Kurhikaueri*, is one of our supreme deities. Fire should always be present in the renewal of cycles, festivities, and a living sense in every one of our traditions and practices. So for us, this presence marks the beginning of a new phase in the community."

The transition to this new phase represented by comunalidad constructed around the parangua also is directly linked to the forest, the source that provides for the manifestation of all that the fire represents and makes possible. It is seen as integral to the community of Cherán, and thus the depredation unleashed against the forest was not only experienced as the destruction of a natural resource but as an attack on the community too. Turning again to Yunuen, she observes, "We have always seen ourselves as part of the territory and not the owners of it, not like the capitalists and their logic. To defend the territory, we defend all that inhabits it—the trees, plants, water, wind, and ourselves as human inhabitants of these lands."

The confluence of the symbolism, culture, history, identity, community, self-defense, and autonomy that has been gained or renewed through the creation of the communal government can perhaps best be illustrated in the transition ceremony that occurs every three years among members of the incoming and outgoing Council of Elders.

> At dawn, before the light of the day, in the area of Tupukatiro, located on San Marcos Hill, at a settlement considered to be the origins of the town ... currently known as Piedra del Toro, the twenty-four *k'eris* [great ones or elders] of the Council of Elders met. Ones who handed over the community's mandate and others who received it, together with a small group of people, including relatives and close friends.

It was a solemn act in a sacred place. Only those invited participated. One day before, the Community Patrol had occupied the location, guarding and preparing it. The ceremony was led by four *nana k'ericha*, wise women of great respect and honorability among the people of Cherán. Their invocations included prayers and songs directed to the guardian spirits of the forest.

Every attendee introduced themselves and explained the reasons for their presence, which were mainly to give continuity to the struggle that began on April 15, 2011, and the desire to maintain the memory of the compañeros who gave their lives for the safety of the people.

After all had participated, the nana k'ericha, carrying holders of burning copal, gave a cleansing to those present, covering them in copal smoke and asking of the spirits protection for all and that they may be guided on the right path.

The nana k'ericha took the staff of command of the P'urhépecha people from the one responsible for guarding it and presenting it at important events. They exposed it to the heat of the fire to purify it while the invocations increased in tone. The staff of command of the P'urhépecha people was returned to the hands of the outgoing Council of Elders, who placed it in the hands of the incoming council.[15]

Following this ceremony, the participants come down from the forest to partake in the marches and festivities described earlier.

The creation of community, intimacy, connection, and unity in struggle along with the building of a communal government quite naturally extends

---

15. Jorge Martínez Aparicio, "San Francisco Cherán. Revuelta comunitaria por la autonomía, la reapropiación territorial y la identidad," *Economía y Sociedad* 31, no. 36 (January–June 2017): 162–63.

to the individual experience of living in Cherán. Even outside the spaces of encounter that the autonomous project is rooted in, their impact is present in the day-to-day life of Cherán's inhabitants.

Among the most evident examples is the sense of safety created by being in community, especially for women. In reflecting on what's changed since 2011, María de la Luz says, "Personally I was a woman with a lot of fear. I didn't know my neighbors, I only said hello to about four people, and I think the whole community was living in insecurity from the loggers and in division from being governed by a political party. Since 2011, everything changed. The fear turned into courage and a desire for a just community for all. I participated in the struggle, and feel committed to the community and thankful for all the support of those who continue helping us in our struggle."

Likewise, Yunuen states that an impact on her life has been to be able "to walk home knowing all is well." She adds, "We feel safe moving about the territory we live in. We know that we are all working toward communal well-being. … The simple fact of walking down the street and when the [Community] Patrol asks you questions, it's for your own well-being, and you can ask them for help instead of being afraid of them like before with the police. [We] trust in our form of government, which we never could in a municipality with political parties. We all take care of one another; we are neighbors, we are family."

In various interviews and documents, members of Cherán noted how this safety through community impacted the lives of so many, such as the children, who can now play freely throughout the town without fear; the youths, who instead of being treated as fodder for political parties, found rebellion and identity in supporting the community's uprising, utilizing their energy and grasp of technology to push it into new spheres, projects, and geographies; the LGBTQ community, which is viewed as an integral part of Cherán and has had members named to positions in the government; and individuals with special needs who have been provided with dignified support and employment through the communal businesses.

Julio beautifully links his personal transformation as a result of serving in the government with the transformation of the community as a whole precisely because of the form of organization it has taken:

> We as a community have organized ourselves differently from others, and this organization allows us to grow as a community, as people. As people we are growing in our ways of thinking, broadening our understanding. Change is not in the community; it's not in the infrastructure, it's not in development. Change is inside of us as people.
>
> I was able to see how this form of government has been changing our way of thinking, how we move in the community, giving importance to issues that we ignored before. I've become more of a compañero, to involve myself more. If I can help, I have to do it, because they are members of my community. One day I'm going to need the help of others. That's the essence of our community, to be humanitarians, to be compañeros. Not just in our work, but in our lives too.
>
> [Before 2011], we had lost something and gave importance to superficial things. But since 2011, we returned to giving importance to these essential issues of our community. And to be proud of what we've been able to achieve and share with the rest of the world. The fact of being in the eye of the hurricane is also a great responsibility: to stay on the path and do the right thing. If we want to be a community free of corruption, we have to make it so. If we want to be a community inclusive of everybody, we have to make it so. I see life differently, through the life of my community."

Cherán has undergone a dramatic change in just a few short years. It is a change that extends to the deepest sense of what it means to be a person living among others within a territory. And that change has been achieved through a community rebellion to remove oppressive systems of violence, be they in the shape of cartels, loggers, police, or politicians and their parties. Yet as Yunuen reminds us, it is important not to forget that this change was accompanied by loss and difficulty. "From these heights, eight years later, one could say it looks easy. But the truth is that it cost lives, many tensions, and eternal hours of collective discussion. At different times during the uprising, several have fallen or been disappeared. The demand for justice continues to ring out and be remembered. Recently, during the commemoration of the eighth anniversary of the uprising, a plaque was placed in the main plaza of the community with the names of the fallen and disappeared. The anger at these losses reminds us that this movement has cost us much, and must be defended and maintained."

Part of maintaining what has been won is identifying the work that remains. Unsurprisingly, the major ongoing concerns are those that still link Cherán to oppressive structures—specifically, as many interviewees mentioned, the reliance on programs and funding from the state, and the arrangement of referring major "anticommunal conduct" to the state prosecutor.

Resolving both those matters are long-term projects, and Cherán realizes it is at the beginning of a long walk. There is a confidence in the structures that residents have built together and the gains that have been achieved in such a short period. Even when there is disagreement, there is trust and patience in the communal government as the mechanism to resolve those. And there is forethought, as in a document quoted by Rodrigo from the first communal government following the 2011 uprising that paints a vision of Cherán in the year 2030:

A Cherán that has recovered and defended an indigenous identity among all sectors and ages. That has resignified being indigenous from a place of dignity and identity. An organized Cherán, supported in networks of solidarity and respect, with a firm focus on strengthening the community. A community with high levels of integration, with participation from the people, with its forest recovered. ... An economically active and balanced municipality, with a wide network of cooperative and communal businesses without the vices of capitalism. A safer Cherán, where social and political stability has allowed for the emergence of tranquility in the population and hope in a better community. With high levels of education, in equilibrium with nature, recovering the indigenous cosmovision of respect and care for mother earth. A Cherán that has reduced or nearly eradicated selfishness among the population; where people have regained trust in one another. In Cherán, political parties have disappeared, we have consolidated the structure and functioning of an alternative political system, based on our usos y costumbres, that makes the existence of political parties something unnecessary, obsolete.

The community of Cherán is well on its way toward meeting those goals. Initiated by a spontaneous uprising, its members undertook a process of reconstructing community, which in turn led to the creation of an autonomous communal government rooted in and beholden to that community. It is a dynamic system designed to administer the needs of the community as dictated by the community itself through the bonfires as well as neighborhood and community assemblies. Yet no less important, the communal government is a process that builds community without the mediation or division of political parties, and to a lesser extent, capitalism and the state. Community and communal government in Cherán are reciprocal processes through which each is fed and strengthened by the other. In a brief time, this has led not only to a municipality that functions on a practical, administrative level but also one that has had a transformative impact on its residents, creating a sense of safety, purpose, identity, and belonging through cooperation and struggle as a community.

It is no wonder that other P'urhépecha communities have bestowed on Cherán the name *Cherán K'eri*, meaning Great Cherán. That recognition has extended far beyond P'urhépecha territory as well, as the echoes of the achievements of this municipality of twenty thousand has resounded within and far outside Mexico. Whether it is seen as an inspiration, guide, or model, it is above all a vibrant, living spark of the liberatory possible in an all-too-desolate landscape.

As Julio observes, "We're aware that along the way, many issues can arise. But it's like a marriage: not everything in life is going to be happiness or good moments. Life is full of highs and lows. And we're going to find ourselves in difficult, complicated moments. But above all, we have to give one another a chance."

*

Scott Campbell is a radical writer and translator based in the so-called United States. For two decades, he has been involved in various forms of solidarity work with social and indigenous movements in the territory referred to as Mexico and beyond. His website is https://fallingintoincandescence.com/. He would like to extend his deep thanks and appreciation to all the community members of Cherán who shared their time, insights, experiences, and knowledge. Special thanks to Yunuen Torres, without whose tireless efforts and endless patience this work would not have been possible.

"Only with You, this Broom Will Fly"

ROJAVA, MAGIC, AND SWEEPING AWAY THE STATE INSIDE US

Dilar Dirik

And one day,

the (r)evolution came.

We held instructions in our mighty hands,

but the blueprints of the new era were pink and green and upside down,

written in a language that none of us could read,

except a mother with three kids on her back and five hiding under her skirt.

"It says," she said,

"don't expect from the gods, whether earthly or heavenly, what you can find
in yourself."

And thus, walked off

the illiterate woman,

to wash her face with the rays of the sun.[1]

A year into the war in Syria, on July 19, 2012, the people in the majority-Kurdish north of the country took over governmental facilities, hoisted their yellow, green, and red flags, and chanting aloud revolutionary music declared, "Revolution in Rojava." Not many years have passed, but enough things have happened since then to fill entire libraries.[2]

---

1. All the epigraph stories were written by me, based on many conversations with women in Rojava.

2. *Editor's note:* This piece was written in mid-2019, and thus doesn't reflect any of the "things [that] have happened since."

A monstrous fascist entity, the so-called Islamic State (ISIS), rose up, conquered vast territories, and fell within years. Yet ISIS only accounts for a small percent of the unimaginable violence, brutality, and trauma inflicted on millions of people by the Syrian forces and other groups involved in the ongoing war, not least of which involves the global arms trade that sponsors and perpetuates conflicts around the world. In a short time, various peoples, communities, cultures, and ecologies suffered irreversible losses. Considering the international system within which all this was able to happen, it seems meaningless to say that it could have been prevented.

Parallel to these atrocities, though, volumes of stories of resistance, courage, and liberation were written, as various communities came together to fight shoulder to shoulder against seemingly invincible doctrines of destruction. In the early 2010s, peoples across the Middle East and North Africa revolted against the authoritarian nation-states that deprived them of the means to live in a dignified and meaningful manner. Like a supernatural force, the spirit of revolution spread as if wildfire from country to country, as hegemonic global powers eagerly tried to suffocate, control, or at least contain it. Within this context, the conditions to declare the revolution in Rojava presented themselves. Although the fight against ISIS was militarily supported by the US-led Global Coalition forces, the people on the ground, notably including the People's Defense Forces (YPG) and Women's Defense Forces (YPJ), had been defending their regions against ISIS and similar groups, backed by the hostile Turkish state, since 2012. In fact, it was their commitment to building a world without such coalitions, without doctrines of power, domination, and exploitation, that enabled the peoples in Rojava to defend their values for a life in freedom. Especially with the battles in places like Kobanê, it became clear to many that what was at stake in this war was not merely the defense of a territory but also a refusal to accept violence and fascism as a fact of life as well as a belief in the possibility of building a different world.

In a world of capitalist assaults on our imagination, dreams, and hopes in the potentiality of alternatives, the idea of revolutionary change and liberated societies may resemble fairy tales in remote places beyond our reach in time and space. It appears as though revolution is something that happens out there, elsewhere, not here, not now, not to us. And yet a decade ago, if you had told the impoverished and colonized Kurdish people in northern Syria that one day internationalists from around the world would be buried in these lands after helping to defend the people's resistance against fascism, who would have believed it?

Sometimes radical imaginaries require that we stretch our temporal and spatial scale just enough to envision the possible, without losing sight of the immense labor and often sacrifice that is required to achieve such possibilities. This is the case when trying to make sense of what has been referred to as the "revolution in Rojava," which over the years came to signify a large-scale sphere of self-determined autonomy not only in the localized absence of a state among some three million people and tens of thousands of square miles of land but also, relatively speaking, outside the control of an international system of domination and exploitation.

Rojavayê Kurdistanê simply means "western Kurdistan" in Kurdish, as it refers to the westernmost area of Kurdistan divided into four parts one century ago. It is within this Rojava, in the context of the Syrian war, that the Kurdish liberation movement's system of democratic confederalism, a political project developed by imprisoned leader Abdullah Öcalan as an alternative to the nation-state, started to be implemented in relative freedom and on a larger scale. While in the past, autonomous structures were built up in northern Kurdistan/Turkey as well in the form of communes, assemblies, congresses, cooperatives, and academies, these efforts were criminalized, banned, and destroyed over the past ten or fifteen years by the state under the Justice and Development Party.

In light of this, since 2011, to present a "third way" in rejection of the two available political options—the regime, or the increasingly radicalizing and foreign-determined opposition—people started to form their nonstate alternative, or self-governance structures. While much of this organizing was shaped by spontaneous and creative responses to the developments in the region, the effect of the forty-year-old legacy of the Kurdistan Workers' Party, led by Öcalan in Rojava, cannot be understated.

At the same time, from reconciliation committees and tribunes, to media work and education, to social and cultural activities, to economic and political decision-making bodies, the women's movement in Rojava is building up its own autonomous confederal system from the bottom up. It's doing so in order to secure women's achievements, interests, and needs in the face of patriarchal violence in their movements, communities, and families. One of the most common phrases that one hears in this political atmosphere is that "the revolution in Rojava is a women's revolution." Indeed, the movement aspires to make women's liberation the defining criterion of the social transformation's success.

In the meantime, balancing the realities of war, diversity of the communities, external attacks, and domestic conflicts as well as sensitivities related to social issues, parallel to the directly democratic practices and educational activities on the ground, a representative federal system was formed over time to allow the region to deal as a coherent unit with outside elements.

Not least due to the ever-changing geopolitical, economic, and social dynamics, what started out as the Democratic Self-Administration of Rojava with three cantons announced in January 2014, has changed in form, size, and shape almost every year ever since. As the war against ISIS spread beyond majority-Kurdish Rojava, in 2016, the term "northern Syria" began to be used exclusively to do justice to the cultural diversity in the region. With the ousting of ISIS from the eastern part of the country, the self-administration came to encompass the Democratic Federation of Northern and Eastern Syria. Today, there are several "regions" with cantons, which have districts, assemblies, city councils, and thousands of communes that govern themselves. While Rojava remains the symbolic name for this liberation project, because it started in the majority-Kurdish areas, as of the end of 2018, the political system of the large area protected by the Syrian Democratic Forces was referred to as the Autonomous Administration of North and East Syria. What it will be called tomorrow is yet to be seen!

The admittedly complex network of movements, self-governance structures, levels of accountability, and decision-making mechanisms appears almost as illegible to bureaucratic state systems as the protective geography of Kurdistan's mountains. As we will see, however, we need to divert our gaze from the drone view to the movement of politics on the grassroots level to make sense of Rojava's social dynamics. This is important especially when considering that one of the main points of argument within radical circles in the past seven years has been the labeling of Rojava as a "revolution." Either clinging onto old-fashioned, memorized formulas on the "how-to" of revolutions, or capitalist views of social transformation and change that expect instant reward and tangible results, many ignored that in the lives of countless people, especially women, thousands of small revolutions started to realize themselves in a collective process.

What if we were to take up a feminist lens when analyzing the efforts of grassroots self-organization? Can we define revolution from a feminist perspective? Is it possible to view revolution as a process that requires patience, care, communality, and leadership that is selfless and productive, aiming at the development of life itself? To keep more witches and their magic from being burned and annihilated, do we need to break the jinx of the state that has so profoundly damaged our relationships, mentalities, and personalities?

Revolution Is Not a Magic Wand . . .

A million years ago, people thought that the stretched index fingers of little boys in Syria and Iraq were taught to them by an army of men, who had come to steal their dreams and loot their futures.

In reality, however, these children were pointing at the sky, trying to spot the flying caravan of magical women in the clouds.

The story goes that one day, in a dark, moldy basement in ar-Raqqa, a group of women from different countries, of different tongues, decided to come together to share their stories, away from the gaze of the male guard with four pairs of eyes and a microphone-shaped beard who was watching them at all times. In those days, whenever women came together to speak about their conditions and lives, society would refer to this as an act of "conspiracy." The moment the women gathered in a circle and faced each other, surrounded by their infant children, they felt as though they had suddenly broken a charm; they felt relieved of the duty to guard an ancient secret.

Bewildered and shocked about this obscene sight of women in assembly, the guard's moustache fell off and landed on his lap. Anxiously trying to pick up the twitching, two-legged moustache, his body suddenly froze in movement. Everyone's heads turned to Ezra, the oldest woman in the basement. The tips of her two white braids were still smoking. They had been the cause of this epic turn of events. Defying her hunched back, she assumed a proud posture to say, "I always knew I had magical powers!"

The awkward pose of the man's stiff body immediately became a play-ground for the children. They climbed up his archaic authority-shoulders, monkey-hanging themselves from these arms of ancient abuse. Whoever was the first to reach his warning index finger won the game round until they abolished winning altogether and just enjoyed themselves.

To antiauthoritarian radicals, the idea that the egalitarian utopias of socialism have been betrayed historically by states and statist mind-sets is nothing new. Anarchists in particular have been attentive to the exploitative nature of the state institution as a tool of domination and hierarchy. Statist notions of socialism stand in contrast to movements and perspectives that rely on the consciousness as well as action of everyday people, and their potential to become subjects of transformative social processes without orders from above. As described by authors like anarchist anthropologist James C. Scott, state socialism's high modernist visions of a bureaucratically governed, socially engineered society imply the notion that a flawless statist order would render politics obsolete. One can add that it would render notions of ethics, justice, or accountability redundant. Why get involved in the messy business of organizing life when anonymous, obscure institutions can gladly take charge?

Despite being critical of the state as an institution, many radicals seem to adopt a mode of understanding society that is not too dissimilar from it, though. The ways in which radicals around the world have struggled to make sense of Rojava is an expression of this phenomenon. Instead of considering the historical, socioeconomic, cultural, and geopolitical context in which Rojava asserted itself as an alternative to existing surrounding systems of exploitation, people seemed to think that lasting societal change could come about with certain magical formulas.

"But you haven't abolished private property!"

"But women are still doing all the housework!"

"But you continue to use so much plastic! What about ecology?"

Ready-made solutions, however, are an expression of a capitalist mode of thought, which demands instant gratification without labor, care, and sustainability. Moreover, one can't help but think that sectarian understandings of anything slightly radical going on anywhere in the world resemble the authoritarianism of abusive patriarchal fatherhood that lacks all self-criticism, and rejects, punishes, and disciplines its child when they do not turn out in one's own image. While expecting rapid change in social relations, this patriarchal notion of revolution, even when referring to itself as capitalist, is in fact employing a view of society as a factory product. Yet fundamental societal transformation is not the same as life in a squat, where one may come across people more or less inclined toward similar politics.

Feminist prefigurative politics, less focused on measurable impact, or provable or testable formulas, but concerned with care, sustainability, collectivism, ecology, and the self-determination and autonomy of different identities, allows us a view of revolution that is different from a fatherlike radical politics that treats society as a group of objects to be disciplined and led. Revolutionary processes require patience and love, hope and belief.

Yet There's Magic in Rejecting the Doctrine of Impossibility

Sahra from east of the river looked west at Zamaan, who looked back at Sahra: "Take my name and let your name be mine." They exchanged names, but remained themselves, became themselves even more deeply, for they had claimed the power to name themselves.

It is possible to imagine flags hung upside down, uniforms worn inside out, and marches sung backward, but it is difficult to imagine a world without hierarchy. Such is authoritarianism's impact on our imaginary. We can only conceive of possibilities through the lens of what we already know, when the logics of our lifeworlds are governed by mechanisms and structures of top-down power. "Capitalist realism," as described by theorist Mark Fisher in his book of that name, refers to the dominant and increasingly hegemonic notion that "not only is capitalism the only viable political and economic system, but also that it is now impossible even to *imagine* a coherent alternative to it."[3]

Many thinkers around the world have pointed out the ways in which the state, especially under capitalism, represents a secular entity with seemingly divine attributes. The power of the state, omnipresent, omniscient, omnipotent—and yes, omnivorous—stifles our movements, thoughts, and sense of self to such an extent that we almost cease to know our own power to act on the world. Dividing our lives into spheres of control and administration (household versus public life, cities versus nature, and so on) is part of the state project to divorce us from our ability to live meaningfully. While rendering itself to be the beginning and end of everything, the capitalist state kills all that about life that it cannot commodify, including our imagination.

In the patriarchal worldview, magic—or rather, illusion—is yet another tool in the authoritarian kit in order to deceive, mislead, and manipulate thoughts, beliefs, and social structures. By way of impressing the subject—a spectator with seemingly unintelligible, inconceivable powers—the illu-

---

3. Mark Fisher, *Capitalist Realism: Is There No Alternative?* (Ropley, UK: Zero Books, 2009), 2.

sionist—that is, the grandiose state—ties the subject to their chair without bonds. Nationalism, fascism, and neoliberalism use similarly deceptive tools, including violence, to claim power over life and death in the earthly world and beyond. Despite being built on pretensions, impositions, and false images, this treacherous system of authoritarian power has a real impact on most people's everyday lives. This power does not create; it only destroys.

While asserting their realities in all spheres of our life through ideology, illusion, and force, both the capitalist state and patriarchy at the same time fundamentally rely on dashing our belief in other forms of seemingly magical power. Mesmerized by the power of the state or father figure, we frequently forget our own power, and our relationship to ourselves, society, and nature. Oftentimes, the reproduction of life through the unpaid emotional and physical work done especially by women appears to us as magic, in a derogatory or at least disbelieving sense. As described by feminist author Silvia Federici in *Caliban and the Witch*, for instance, the capitalist logic of work needed to drive out any notion of magic from people's lives in order to monopolize reality. The power over life and death could not be left to instances of power outside the state, whether material or imagined.

According to twentieth-century anarchist anthropologist Pierre Clastres, in Western philosophy, society is inherently connected to the notion of people living under a state, which in turn considers itself to be the center of society. Thus, state societies refer to nonstate societies as "people without faith, without law, without king," or in other words, nonsocieties. The glorification of the state as the supreme instance of secular sovereignty has been a crucial assumption since the Enlightenment era and especially since the formulations of Georg Wilhelm Friedrich Hegel, whose rationalist dialectics further strengthened the foundations of a modernist paradigm that understands the state as a logical step in humanity's linear progression toward an enlightened order. Among nonstate peoples, however, in Clastres's view, the political does not exist in a sphere external to the self in the sense that it is not delegated to a statist "other" outside society but instead operates through and within society. In short, the political sphere cannot be separated from the social sphere.

But the magic of life lingered in the shadows. It is now strongly connected to what could be called the principle of hope; it allows us to imagine that the course of things can go differently. Magic breaks with the doctrine of impossibility, or the hegemonic slogan of late capitalism that "there is no alternative." The realm of magic is a world protected from the constraints imposed on us by statist ideology, heteropatriarchal mentalities, religious dogmas, and capitalist mutilations of our fantasies, and a way to try to counter their concrete assaults.

Seen in this light, statelessness or antistate modes of organizing in fact lend themselves to direct ways of intervening in and acting on life. They protect and defend a piece of the magical world outside the state and patriarchy by embodying alternatives through their very existence and ways of life.

An ecological view of life, divorced from the statist-patriarchal gaze, will allow us to understand that just as we cannot fully grasp the materiality of magic, we cannot prefiguratively imagine liberated individuals outside societal contexts. The magic happens in the actually doing of the alternative itself.

The guardian's keys, shaped like body parts, were seized by Lenya, who had never been behind a wheel, but knew all about driving nonetheless. As the women and children entered the bus one by one, Lenya hungrily eyed the driver's seat like her baby had done to her breast, until . . .

With a devout "Bismillah!" she heaved her heavy body onto her new throne. Her manic laugh, as she maneuvered the bus through the sky, had a blue color and kept evil patriarchal spirits away from her precious passengers.

Despite its aspiration to become a sphere in which freedom can develop, on top of being encircled by violence, Rojava also faces all the sorts of problems that any other context around the world does when it comes to organizing. How do we even begin to motivate a severely traumatized, mainly conservative, impoverished society, whose homes and dreams have been taken away?

Parallel to processes and efforts to create new ways of relating to one another, there are of course large sections of society that are apolitical, disinterested, or otherwise preoccupied. And within Rojava, there are also hundreds of thousands of internally displaced people and refugees with urgent needs to be met in an efficient manner.

If we look at the context in which Rojava's revolution emerged, we will see more clearly that what the people on the ground are up against is not only an army of different systems of violence and authority but also a whole set of internalized mentalities as a result of oppression and colonization. The following is a testimony by female revolutionary Fouwza Yousif, whom I interviewed in Rojava:

Unlike other parts of Kurdistan, Syrian policy toward the Kurds was determined by a policy of "de-identification." Not only was Kurdish identity denied, the state also wanted to render people landless. By stripping many people of their citizenship, the state took away any possible Arab identity and treated Kurds like landless foreigners. The right to buy and own a house, land, property, and businesses, all of which are basic things for people's economy in this region, were denied. One had to register someone else's name.

The impact of the existence as a landless, rootless people went deeper than political denial. Psychologically, those who still had Syrian IDs feared that if they rose up, their rights as citizens would be taken away as well. When Arabs were settled in the fertile, majority-Kurdish areas, Kurds were separated from each other, and a grudge developed toward the state, but also toward these Arab tribes. In legal disputes, the government usually sided with Arabs; law was politicized.

While pitting communities against each other, the state further implemented a state-of-emergency rule in the area to check and control the Kurds. The state policy was based on intelligence, by turning the population into agents. Communal ties were broken as people were increasingly afraid to trust each other. Although people spoke Kurdish at home, the language was forbidden in the public realm. Students were encouraged in school to tell on their own families if they spoke Kurdish.

Since only Syrian citizens could become officers, young Kurds lacked incentives for studying. Education served as a tool of assimilation anyway. There was no mention of the Kurds in the Syrian syllabus; geography and history were distorted. Êzîdî people were forced to study Islam in schools. Those who did not receive education remained ignorant, and those who did study became assimilated.

Economically, the state tried to tie the economy of this fertile, rich area to its central administration, putting the people in a state of dependency. You could only grow things like wheat and lentils. Due to real socialist policy, there were no private sectors anyway. Nothing was planned according to the needs of the society, but instead organized for state interests, although the resources

were plentiful and could have fed everyone. Oil would be extracted from
Rimelan, but refined in Homs. Wheat would be grown in Cizîrê and Kobanê,
but milled in Aleppo, Homs, or Damascus. It was a biopower regime, an economic special war strategy, a state between death and life; people would be
given barely enough to survive, not to live comfortably. It was a colonial treatment to leave people hungry and dependent. Landless as they were, without
industry, people migrated to Damascus and Aleppo.

Finally, there was no chance to organize; even cultural or social centers
were banned. Existing ones either operated secretly, or remained insignificant
and marginal. The secret service was so strong that associations were infil-
trated and could not do meaningful, serious work. Trade unions and civil society organizations? Zero. All had to adhere to Ba'ath, at least through affili-
ation. There was no real civil society. All this resulted in an organizationless,
landless, tongueless, identityless society.

In this sense, there were several layers of exploitation that affected
people in a variety of ways. With the revocation of citizenship and economic policies, the Kurds were psychologically made to feel like guests in
their homes, impeding the development of a rage against the system, due
to a lack of identification with the land. Military marches, glorifications of
Arab nationalism, and gratifying encouragement to join the Ba'ath party accompanied the absence of teachings on Kurdish history and existence to
ideologically enable exploitation. In parallel, the assimilation and dispossession policies from the 1960s onward were seen by many as a preemptive
attempt to reward potential opposition in the Arab community with Kurdish lands, causing nationalist sentiments on both sides to pit groups against
each other that might otherwise challenge the state.

That the greatest revolution is the one against the ways in which authoritarianism manifests itself in one's own personage is also evident in

another testimony. The following words belong to Kînem, a spokesperson at the Asayish academy in Rimelan:

> The Syrian regime tried to destroy a people by nothing-izing it. It didn't use genocide and direct violence like in Turkey and Iraq. But it created an alienated, extinguished society that was rendered dreamless. This society was conditioned to accept its degraded state as its state of nature.
>
> In this sense, our greatest struggle has been in the realm of personalities. People here had no life dream, no life utopia, left to hold onto; they found excuses to justify backwardness. The culture of laziness and lying was dominant. People learned to be secretive and almost automatically lie in the face of difficulty, as though the regime was in front of them. They still can't believe the regime is gone. This demonstrates the psychological dimensions of the system's expressions within the individual.
>
> Combined with an alienated relationship to work and dispossession from one's own land, this wretched state established a notion of nonbelonging and thus nonresponsibility to public life. If you are given drops of water in a desert, you find yourself in a state between life and death that will cause you to appreciate the most oppressive regime. In this sense, the mental revolution is truly the most difficult part of the revolutionary process. It is easy to liberate lands; it is not easy to liberate people from the poverty of slave mentalities.

On Breaking the Statist Jinx

The new Zamaan spread her arms, and more fabric than was already covering her body fell out from underneath her armpits. With a skilled movement, she pushed herself off the ground. She was flying; her veil was her wings. "I will be your guide in the sky. I see, I understand. I protect through knowing."

In the meantime, the new Sahra, sitting on top of the bus, silently recited forbidden fairy tales in the rhythm of the wind in her grayed hair.

Farzana, beside her, caught a tree branch, hurling through the wind. As she uttered a prayer-like recital, her scarred fingertips turned the branch three times until it became a string instrument that the musicians of the world had yet to see. Her ears on Sahra's poetry, she played a song that silenced the thunderstorm around them.

The first written law codex emerged in the twenty-first century BC, issued by the first states and institutionalized patriarchal systems. Several hundred kilometers north along the Euphrates River, in the twenty-first century AD, women drafted laws of nonstate people's democracies, while questioning assumptions of law, justice, and authority. The justice system of Rojava aims to create an ethical-political society with the means of solving its own problems and managing its affairs. This raises the question of the origin of authority, power, rights, and legitimacy. Does justice mean equal treatment before law, regardless of the individual and society's conditions? Is adherence to law contrary to revolutionary principles and practices? Can a system be nonstatist and have the "authority" to write "law" and create a system of "justice"?

When I interviewed her, Rufend Xelef, a young woman from Tirbêspiyê, was the copresident of the legislative council of the Cizîrê Canton. She had been part of the work for the social contract of Rojava (published in January 2014) and women's laws. Having been trained in law at a university under the regime, she spoke of an ongoing struggle to overcome internalized state mentalities, which the initial committee discussed for weeks. There are several layers and systems of justice and law that cooperate, coordinate, and counterbalance each other in an attempt to politicize society, while allowing for adaptations to a radical democratic system. Several legal documents coexist alongside the people's tribunals, people's and women's houses (*mala gel* and *mala jin*, respectively), and commune-linked peace and reconciliation (*silhê*) committees.

In the early years of the revolution, to ensure a sense of stability and prevent the traumatized society from descending into arbitrariness, the need emerged to establish a justice system. In the first instance, peace and reconciliation committees aimed to facilitate the communes' autonomous solving of their problems without interference from strangers. If a dispute is not resolved in the commune, the case is taken to the mala gel or mala jin of the town. These committees listen to the relevant parties, write down all sides of the story, stamp the files, and send them to the tribunal in the last instance. As Rufend explained,

> As oppressed people, we automatically think of violence, when we think of law and state. When we studied law in the state system, we could not find any justice, any solution to social problems, because the law was far from society's reach. Our own rights were violated. Our new system originates from the people and tries to serve them. The legislation is not created to take food away from people or protect state power. We constantly remind ourselves that we don't write these laws for a small group of privileged people but rather for the comfort and happiness of society.

I met Rufend for the first time during my stay in June 2015 at the women's academy in Rimelan, where she was part of several committees traveling around to discuss the women's laws with large sections of society. At the time of our interview, she was part of the committee to establish a new justice council.

> People said, "How dare you come up with laws? Who are you to do that?" Placing their hopes in the state that oppressed them, people kept wanting to return to state authority. Particularly jurists were upset when we proposed to

create people's tribunals with nonexperts on the judging board. They said people are not educated and don't know what they do, but that they themselves had studied law and were state authorized to practice it. But how much of society's problems were they aware of? Did they realize how far their own ways of deciding and judging were from the way things work in society?

Rather than aspiring to uphold a "blind," objective justice ideal that treats all cases in a standardized, identical manner, whereby parties are judged to be guilty or innocent, accuser or accused, the aim is to achieve consensus. The logic is to end hostility and resolve underlying issues at the root of disputes to assure lasting peace and reconciliation. While there are guidelines, there is no standard sentencing, as each case is treated within an individual context. According to Rufend, around 70 percent of the cases get resolved at the commune and council levels before they reach the courts, while about six thousand court cases reach the canton level every year. The system renders obsolete the identity of the lawyer as the protector of state-sanctioned law by making citizens the mediators of justice, whereby societal analysis, knowledge of a community's issues, emotional sensitivity, and commitment to ethical principles is prioritized over bureaucracy and law. The system's manifold structures and levels of accountability and answerability allow for focused, indeed sociological analyses, whereby the people working in the field of justice identify the diversity of social problems in relation to their geographic, historical, cultural, and economic dimensions. For instance, while oil-rich cities and areas close to the border report higher numbers of oil theft and smuggling, large cities like Qamishlo face human trafficking. Therefore each region must find its own formats and approaches to assuring justice. Since most crimes are related to the economy, the need for a just economic system arises. Rufend describes some of the difficulties of abolishing state-referencing mentalities:

The main problem was that fundamentally we believed that only the state has the power to legislate. We kept returning to the statist framework, although the state was the reason for our revolution. We needed to understand that the state could not be the authority to "give" rights. How to write laws for a new system, with a new philosophy? The revolution had started, but the state mentality was still present. Our reflexes against authority had been killed by the state. Actionism was dead. So much that we were doing things without knowing why. This lack of awareness or internalization of behaviors was reflected in our discussions. We asked, Whose justice are we protecting? Whose rights? Where do law, rights, and justice come from?

Rufend gave examples of men fearing a loss of rights with the women's laws. The women's laws are not seen as solutions in themselves but rather serve as blueprints for general principles to prevent things such as underage marriages, bride exchanges, polygamy, and violence. Educational seminars accompany the process to promote radical principles while not losing touch with societal realities, which would otherwise cause backlash, rejection, and hostility. The tribunal is a platform, attended by different parties, including delegates from the umbrella women's movement Kongreya Star—which is organized in the form of a congress—peace and reconciliation councils, martyr's families, and community members, who get to voice their perspectives and ask questions.

According to people who work in this field, society gets judged whether a mentality, historical condition, or social problem is being interpreted. Was the person forced to do this? Do they regret their act? Did they steal to survive or exploit others? How can this person be helped? What needs to change for this crime to stop? In this sense, not only the person who feels harmed, but the whole society suffers from each issue, which is why the ancient "eye for an eye" philosophy of law is not a solution in a nonstate system. The origin of crime and violence is delegated to the existence of predominant but historically established "mentalities" instead of being taken for granted. Against a Hobbesian assumption of the inherently corrupt nature of humans, a rehabilitative, reconciliatory approach to the ills of society emerges, strengthened by the extent to which the newly developing system can deliver its promises of liberation and solidarity.

Mobilizing the Tools to Struggle

Sitting in a circle with the children of the women, Ranya sang a song from the women of her tribe in the desert. In the open palm of her hands, the children could see the reflection of the universe. Each scar of her large body taught them another lesson about beauty, life, and death. Nobody was there to police her knowledge. Every child that she blessed with a kiss from her wisdom-speaking lips was embarking on a trip to the school of life.

There are a variety of mechanisms to guide the democratization process in Rojava; alongside the communes, committees, assemblies, congresses, and cooperatives, a complex system of documents, principles, guidelines, formal and informal practices, silent agreements, and economies all impact how decisions are taken. Social contracts, oaths, promises, traditions, and dreams all inform the ways in which ethics and politics are woven into each other to create a new social fabric based on justice. As Leyla, a young woman from Tirbêspiyê who experienced a violent and vulnerable childhood, described it, "Before the revolution, we did not have the tools to struggle. Now we start to get to know ourselves and organize the power to struggle."

In the first years of the revolution, hundreds of communes and assemblies were formed. The community houses now each solve dozens of issues in their communities every month. As observed by many, one of the main reasons for this efficiency is the absence of bureaucracy. Instead of being driven by formalities and legal proscriptions, people act spontaneously and according to collective notions of justice.

Through their involvement in cooperative economic efforts, women especially have become increasingly more aware of their abilities. They are less likely to accept exploitation now that they have taken charge of their own economy and self-organization.

At the mala jin, younger and older women work together for the first time on equal terms—a challenge to the gerontocracy that is a deeply rooted mechanism of power and hierarchy in the regional culture. Rather than erasing differences of age, it has encouraged older female workers to keep an open mind about new perspectives, while the youths benefit from the former's life experiences.

Although each canton runs its economy independently, committees oversee the intercanton economy and manage their coordination based on solidarity. This way, for instance, the majority of humanitarian aid for the cantons of Kobanê and Afrîn came from Cizîrê. Rojava was not only spared from famine but also managed to look after hundreds of thousands of internally displaced persons from Syria and refugees from Iraq. Although the war economy due to the external and internal embargo on Rojava made everything more expensive, the prices for goods have continuously remained much lower than in the rest of Syria, and because of that, many people who initially left Rojava to live in Turkey or Iraqi Kurdistan have now returned. In what's referred to as the "democratic autonomy" system, the aim is to create economic alternatives, relying mostly on the development of cooperatives. The oppressiveness of the long-term conditions of war is manifested in the constant balance between keeping the war economy going, assuring the basic needs of millions of people, struggling to uphold principles, and planning and establishing a farsighted system against exploitation and for economic justice.

Key to this is the plethora of autonomous women's media outlets in Rojava. Whether TV programs, women-only studios, or publications, their aim is to bring an antipatriarchal perspective to light. These media both increase the visibility of women's active roles and work in the revolution as well as create news from an autonomous women's viewpoint with the goal of transforming ideas in society in general. Apart from the technical training (news writing, editing, camerawork, personal computer skills, reporting, and so on), women train to develop an eye that is sensitive to sexism and patriarchy. It is a priority to focus on the untold or invisible stories of women's daily lives, political struggles, practical work, and history. This includes altering the language and formats in which TV discussions are held. According to Jiyan, one of the coordinators of Ragihandina Jinê (RAJIN), the women's media association,

> Before the revolution, opposition could be arrested or killed for expressing their thoughts. People relied on the state to get information and knowledge of the world. This is one way in which sexism and chauvinism were naturalized—through media. In our education, we research the media's role in the creation of oppressive and violent systems. For the creation of a society, a conscientious media is necessary. Around the world, media plays a role in justifying wars, causing friction between communities, and glorifying violence, especially against women. They do not solve society's issues. We show that people can and do coexist; that women do struggle. We report about efforts of peace, freedom, and coexistence in practice.

The idea is to question dominant assumptions about the seemingly natural course of events and transform narratives, as told through the eyes of the oppressed. Women's media becomes an intervention in the ways in which daily events are communicated:

When a woman commits suicide, it is often due to the violence she experienced, but society claims that she must have breached traditional norms, violated family honor, and so on. In other words: she deserved it. We try to understand the wider social, political, and even historical contexts of such issues. What kind of society do we live in, where a woman is driven to suicide? Instead of saying, "A woman killed herself," we focus on the fact that a woman has been murdered or driven to death by an existing antiwoman system that normalizes violence. It is not an individual act but rather a mentality, a system, that did this. We try to write differently, to expose social contradictions and change dominant perceptions. Women see themselves or women like themselves on the screen, accomplishing all sorts of things that previously were taboo. That becomes your self-defense. This consciousness becomes a weapon to you, with which you then know how to act and stop taking certain things for granted.

Apart from a new general educational system, a communal education through the new academies has been developed in Rojava. The ideological and political motivation behind it is less concerned with teaching knowledge and facts; instead, it's about creating subjects who can think for themselves, and have the ability to be active politically and solve issues in their own society. Education is viewed as vital in defending the self against assimilation, alienation, and consumption by capitalist modernity's physical and metaphysical weapons. Moreover, revolutionary principles such as women's liberation and solidarity between peoples cannot be expected to come naturally in a historically oppressed community also traumatized by war. In the words of Adnan Husên, who was teaching at the Mesopotamia Academy for Social Sciences at the time I interviewed him,

It is relatively easy to achieve a military or political revolution using force by taking advantage of temporary conjunctural moments, but in light of colonialist politics, if a long-term and sustainable transformation with practical outcomes is aspired to, the revolution must start in the minds. It might look like a contradiction that while we are amid war, with embargoes as well as political and military attacks from all sides, we are sitting in a room, discussing history. But we have no alternative to this.

The development of a different consciousness complements the military aspects of this revolution. Otherwise, the self-defense aspect will not hold meaning in itself; military victories alone will not achieve ideals. Without consciousness, awareness, and knowledge, all sacrifices quickly disappear. If you call your war a revolution, for it to be more than the change of a shell, it must be filled with revolutionary content for society, based on a democratic, ecological, and women's liberationist paradigm. To work toward a farsighted perspective for the liberation of society, the revolutionary principles must be socialized.

Twenty-year-old Nujîn, whose class I attended at the academy, explained the pedagogical process as a means of finding one's voice while acting on societal processes:

It's about understanding the conditions and situations you find yourself in. To know and understand yourself is an old human endeavor. Here, we create the possibility of thought. This place creates its own teachers. We haven't reached a professional stage, and we don't say that we are "experts" in anything. It's not like the state created a university for me to visit. I myself created this academy [with others]!

For example, we started a discussion in class about the links between the fact that both women's and Kurdish history have not been written. I realized then how history and sociology go hand in hand. In discussions, we analyzed our internalized behaviors. Women at the beginning felt too embarrassed to get up and speak. They were ashamed, having always been taught to sit prettily and shut up. Men were the ones to have opinions. To understand why my own community has certain problems, I need to look at its history and put it into a wider context. And suddenly, when we do this, we realize that we are writing history too!

The academies are neither schools of dogmatic indoctrination nor objective, formal, bureaucratic institutions. They, too, are institutions that emerged out of an identified need to develop deliberative skills to enable active participation in public life. Through raising their consciousness about structures of injustice, people, especially women, realize that their oppressed status is not set in stone but instead can be changed. Especially women with little or no formal education benefit from the academies, which enable them to learn, self-reflect, share experiences, and come up with new concepts of knowledge based on grounded, lived experiences. Their practices that had been dismissed by capitalist, statist, and patriarchal structures are now valued and revived as valid forms of knowing.

Not a Fairy Tale, But a Million Real Stories

Tara, who had been feeling ashamed and unclean the whole day, since she discovered blood in her underwear in the morning and knew that this was a sign of things only getting worse from now on, lifted the ends of her long dress, swirled through the bus, jumping from seat to seat. Every spot that her blood touched began to sprout flowers in different colors: marigolds, poppies, tulips, and daffodils:

"I create, I become. I am myself precisely through changing! It is through me that life can be!"

Whereas at the start, revolutionaries from around the world paid visits to Rojava either to get a firsthand idea of the process or join in any capacity without necessarily having clear plans, today internationalists are physically building their commune in Derîk, learning Kurdish, educating themselves, and participating in the civil structures, often with the aim of eventually returning home to organize. The participation of different ethnic and religious communities in the new system is so common that people do not find it necessary to mention it explicitly anymore. And visually, it is harder to distinguish between seasoned revolutionaries and the local people who have been involved in the public process over the last years, as their levels of knowledge, experience, and confidence increased with the developments on the ground.

Rojava is flourishing in various ways. Street art decorates the walls. Across the region, newly formed centers for theater, cinema, music, dance, and fine arts have been established, recruiting from and performing for local communities, displaced peoples, and refugees. The women's cultural movement Kevana Zerrîn (Golden Crescent) organizes trainings and activities autonomously in cultural centers. Common themes in arts performances are war, peace, coexistence, women's liberation, and resistance to oppression. There are many bands that include several nationalities and perform revolutionary songs in multiple languages.

It is also still a place where a woman can learn about women's history and go home to beat her child for something that is "shameful"; where men can talk publicly about gender equality and yet complain about the increasing divorce cases filed by women; where someone can be part of creating the YPJ and then decide to become a housewife; or where parents gladly defend the land to death, but send their children to Europe.

Yet it is region where many taboos have been broken, forcibly destroyed practices of self-sufficiency have now been remembered and revived, and people don't just aspire to reinstitute the past but rather to do better. As an imam, a religious scholar, explained his understanding of the women's revolution in Rojava to me,

Entire families take part in the revolutionary process today. People see the fruits of their labor, and escape the previous state of misery and poverty. *Jin, jiyan, azadî* ["Women, life, freedom," the main slogan of the Kurdish women's movement] became a philosophy of life here. The women's struggle attracted people from around the world. Kobanê became one of the best-known Syrian cities, due to women's resistance. Of course, this impacts society here when people see the values that were fought for so that we can live.

Mantra-like repetitions of slogans. "Jin, jiyan, azadî." "The Rojava revolution is a women's revolution." Such magical spells, repeated, enacted, and died for, have over time become principles to live by. They are not propaganda for the outside world. Instead, they serve to remind people of the achievability of their own dreams.

In a world in which social entanglements are being forcibly broken up, where ancient ecosystems are being devastated and degraded into nothingness, where our connection to the past and the multitude of presents is being commodified, caricatured, and made alien to us, where bonds between fascist systems and institutions are strangling the lungs of life ever more tightly—it is obvious that the survival of Rojava and other emancipatory projects, no matter the scale, relies on liberatory developments in other parts of the world. This can be seen, for instance, in the catastrophic war in Afrîn, where the Turkish state and its second-largest NATO army attacked the area from the air in support of its local extremist mercenaries, which led to the eventual displacement of close to half a million people. Years of building grassroots structures, local economies, and self-governing systems were destroyed with the silent approval of the international community. Rojava's contribution to our understanding of social struggles is manifold, but one of its most concrete reiterations is the realization that no liberation can exist in a vacuum. Furthermore, liberationist endeavors cannot be preplanned, fully organized to the last detail. Rather, most of the issues that need to be addressed come about during periods of struggle and experimentation. Revolutionary work and internationalist solidarity in this way relate to each other, just as does radical theory and practice. Sometimes we will only gain sight of the so-called next step when we decide to act. And to the extent to which our communities as well as our internationalisms diversify through self-determined and autonomous action, we can liberate ourselves on our own terms, without reliance on formats imposed on us.

Magic is not to be found in the palaces, military bases, or temples of the rulers, who can only delude us into subjugation. Magic *is not really* magic but instead the joyful power to determine our own lives, to speak, define, and decide for ourselves; it is hidden within our potentialities to express our creativity and autonomy hand in hand with other people. Not with guidebooks, but with rooted sight in our daily lives, in connection with the oppressed peoples around the world, in constant warfare against the state within ourselves, we build the worlds that render life meaningful and dignified. Defending these endeavors before fascism suffocates us, before it convinces us again that "there is no alternative," is therefore one of the main tasks for radicals today. To protect Rojava's universal appeal to all those who believe in self-determined life, we must be able to see our struggles in each other. As the Kurdish women's movement asserts, abstractly speaking about "giving" each other solidarity is no longer sufficient if we want to combat, much less defeat, fascism. We need common vocabularies and common perspectives; we need to find ways of struggling together, defying those borders that we've magically been taught to believe in by the state and patriarchy.

And so the flying caravan of magical women exploded notions of time and space, as they set off to explore a revolution on their own terms, on their own time, on their own scale.

At the doorstep of a curious place called Rojava, a woman was sweeping the floor with her broom.

She continued her chore, but with a smile.

"I don't know what you have been told about our country.

But here I am, indeed, running a household."

She stopped her deed and looked up.

"For years, I have been waiting for you, my sisters,

to join me for our next assembly meeting.

Without you, nobody could continue.

Only with you, this broom will fly."

*

Dilar Dirik is a sociologist and activist of the Kurdish women's movement in Europe. She occasionally writes for international outlets on freedom struggles in Kurdistan. Her political work focuses on establishing links between the Kurdish women's liberation movement and women's struggles around the world. Dilar would like to thank all the women who opened their doors and lives to her, and without whom this chapter would not have been possible.

Pirate Ships, Stormy Seas, and Finding Solid Ground

THE QUARTIER LIBRE

DES LENTILLÈRES

Natasha King

It's one o'clock in the afternoon, on a hot, late summer day in 2017, and more than two-thirds of the eighty or so residents of the Quartier Libre des Lentillères are gathered on the grass, eating together, by the wooden-pallet pirate ship that stands mast at the top end of our place. It's only the second time in the nine-year history of this occupation of a piece of old agricultural land in Dijon, France, that the people living here specifically have gotten together to talk. The fact that so many people have turned out is a sign that this moment is urgent and relevant.

There are three broad themes: feelings about this place, practical thoughts about how we live together, and thoughts about collective involvement. People had been invited to write down and put their comments on these themes into three boxes, anonymously, in advance. The three women who are facilitating the meeting (who know the Lentillères well, but don't live here) read each paper aloud from the first box. They speak in French, but there are direct translations taking place in Arabic, Tamasheq/Tuareg, English, and Polish.

People hear other inhabitants express that they are happy and proud to live here. There are comments about people's need to be together and the feeling of being like a big family; the sense of a loss of confidence in and fear of judgment from each other; discomfort over cliques; burnout and a lack of recognition of the work done here; and loneliness.

There are suggestions, too, about getting better at transmitting the history of this place to newcomers; organizing more events that bring us all together; clarifying the uses of collective space; and better recognizing how for some, provocative political action that could result in police repression is not an option. In all this, there is a notable difference between those who speak of "us" and those who speak from "I."

The atmosphere is quiet and thoughtful. There is an intimacy that comes from sharing our feelings and opinions on life together. There is also a sense of relief at being honest and heard.

What has been shared leads to a discussion about racism. Someone wants to know why it is that all the white people here have comfortable living situations while the twenty or so Tuareg who came to live here a few months before do not. For them, it's a clear example that systemic racism exists here. Those people of color who are present—almost half—are asked to confirm this.[1] When they disagree, the meeting descends into shouting and desperation. The accusers leave, disgusted. The rest remain, but are stunned and silent. The silence brings the meeting to a close, six hours after it started.

A few months later, we begin the research project that became this chapter.[2] It's midwinter 2018. The heavy heat of last summer has passed,

---

1. Not that all Europeans are white, of course, or that all non-Europeans are non-white, but three-quarters of the people living here are from places other than Europe, and all of them are people of color too.

2. The project lasted approximately four months, and two of us—both residents of Lentillères—did this research. We conducted interviews, frequently in small groups, with eighteen people, two of whom were ex residents, and sixteen of whom still live here. There are people whose voices are not included in this project, most notably people who are involved in the space but don't live here as well as people who live or garden in what is called the "little Lentillères," a less developed area of land within the site that is often unintentionally yet nonetheless left out of collec-

and a still and gray cold has taken its place. We conduct interviews with small groups of people living here. The conversations are heavy with memories of events from the summer just gone. The meeting described above was part of that, as was the debut of a series of meetings that were themselves intense. These meetings were essentially about racism, but were shaped by a whole bunch of traumatic events—accusations of sexual assault, fights, and a suicide—that took place that year, creating a knot that few people still know how to unravel. There is still a sense of shared pain that we haven't talked about and have barely begun to process. There is for some a lingering sense that the energy in this community right now is somehow bad. As one resident of several years put it, "There are things going around, and I don't know how to act. . . . People don't feel so comfortable here anymore."

This text started with that meeting at the pirate ship because for many, it was the beginning of a collective process that instilled both pride (over almost-complete direct democracy, which in turn strengthened many people's sense of being part of something together) *and* disappointment (because it failed to really move or solve anything, and instead fell back on poorly functioning forms of collective justice that broke people's commitment to the process in the end). It is important to remember that it was an

---

tive activities. Those people who, for many reasons, have either chosen or somehow been forced to leave the Lentillères were also not included. The opinions expressed in this text are therefore those of the people who have managed to stay, and not those who for whatever reason felt they had to leave. And these opinions are filtered through the lenses of the two of us who did this research. As such, it is a flawed attempt at a collective research process. Yet the flaws and successes of collective processes are partly what this anthology is about after all.

exceptional moment, where there was a burst of energy to experiment with and invest in the ways we communicate together. But despite being exceptional, it highlights the utopia we always face in our organizing: reaching toward and falling short of a state of total nonhierarchy. It highlights well the discomfort that comes from partly succeeding and partly failing.

How did we get to this point? To understand, we need to go back a bit and explain a little more about who this community is, and how we arrived at this moment of pride and desperation.

Who Are "We"?

We live in the Quartier Libre des Lentillères. The direct translation is "the free neighborhood of the lentil garden." This place has long been horticultural land, and today it is one of the only remaining parcels of green in the city (although whether any lentils were ever grown here, nobody knows). Around eighty people currently live here, although maybe twice that number are connected and committed to this place.

Ten years ago, in 2009, the Lentillères—La Friche, "the gardens"—was just an abandoned parcel of land with a number of derelict houses and buildings on it, though it would be hard to say that it was ever completely deserted. Like many ignored and apparently useless spaces, it was still occupied by those who either had no choice but to, or else chose to, be in a space that fell under the radar.

Ten years ago, brambles and climbing plants overran the handful of neglected farmhouses and broken walls. The open fields were still tall with shrubs and colonizing trees when a few people started to recultivate some of the land.

But it was a demonstration in Dijon in 2010, organized by a broad coalition of anarchist, leftist, and citizens' groups in the city, that led to the occupation and cultivation of a large parcel of that land, in essence launching the Lentillères. Over time, a sense that there was some life reemerging and connecting began to grow. More intentional activities sprung up, solidifying the Lentillères as a project that saw itself as a struggle to both preserve this green space in the city and prefigure a form of urban collective life that is autonomous from the state. Le Pot'Col'le, the original collective growing project that spearheaded the birth of the free quarter, farms this land still. Over the years, people from the neighborhood have made thirty or so of their own small allotment gardens here too. In 2012, people brought another large parcel of land into cultivation, and it is now the heart of this space. Today the free quarter covers a space of around seven hectares, with intentionally permeable, if distinct and defined, borders.

And over time, more and more people came to live here. At first people occupied the already-existing buildings. In an effort to evict the occupants, the city council destroyed some of these structures. Meanwhile, other buildings came under occupation. People started to add their own structures too. Cabins were constructed, caravans moved in, and yurts were erected. Other spaces were built: a bike workshop, a meeting space, spaces for storing equipment and tools, and a garage. This growth hasn't been totally linear. There were periods when there was a population boom as this place accommodated different groups of people. Five years ago, we were thirty. A year ago, we were almost a hundred.

There have been times when we have had to fight to stay here. We are, after all, a squat. We continue to fight to preserve this land as a green space in the city because we are threatened with plans to build a mixed-housing development, which the city council refers to as an "eco-quarter," on this site. Today the first phase of this project has nearly been realized; next to us now, there is a concrete neighborhood newly decorated with potted trees. The irony that we who wish to resist a rampant form of urbanism face eviction from a supposed eco-quarter paved in the finest asphalt is not lost on us.

Indeed, the visible, public reason for our being here is to preserve this agricultural land and resist the unbridled "development" of the city of Dijon. But this place has always been a hybrid of wants and needs. There are those who came because of political reasons—people from anarchist and leftist milieus, let's say. Then there are those who came here out of practical need, such as people living on the streets because of addiction, immigration issues, or other reasons. For many, these things overlap. It's rarely the case that people live here just for political reasons and not for practical, everyday ones as well.

This diversity means that we are and have always been many different collectives here, and many different "we's." Currently there are ten different residential collectives, and numerous collectives that use or are connected to this space in some way (such as three gardening groups, one bike workshop collective, one well-being collective, and various entertainment collectives).

What Keeps Us Here

We have changed a lot, ultimately growing in size, and what has emerged among us (or was inherited by us), largely organically, is a kind of ethic or basic set of values. These are the things we can say we share, the things that we agree are worth guarding, and the things that make living here so special.

Perhaps the first value is this diversity of ours. Some of us are from rich backgrounds, and others are from the streets. We vary in age from six months to our sixties. Although it was predominantly French in the beginning, most of us who live here now are not from France. Now we come from fifteen different countries, and speak eleven different languages. And from the start, there was a strong connection between this place and the struggle of migrants of different kinds. La Friche has regularly been a temporary home to hundreds of migrants after they have faced eviction from other squats in the city. People living here have worked together many times to confront and resolve these evictions by opening new squats, and those squats have stayed connected to La Friche. In recent years, this place has become the permanent home for some of those who were evicted or displaced from other housing. Most notably, in 2015, a new squat here of people mostly from North Africa was opened, and in 2017, a group of around twenty Tuareg decided to live here after attempts to open a new squat failed. So all this diversity is not in theory. As one resident, who also tends a garden here, put it, "I'm proud of the Friche. It's a great achievement. . . . The fact that we live with asylum seekers is really rare. We really share daily life. We share the same toilet, shower, meal."

This diversity also means that how we see this place as a site of struggle, and who it is that we struggle with and what for, are in turn diverse. The diversity is frequently played out in how we try to live our lives together and the issues we face every day. One resident who has been heavily involved in antifascist organizing felt that "here there is really a lot of struggles that are linked, to me, especially in the way we behave together in daily life, like in economic ways, ecological ways, I don't know how to say it, but an antiracist way. So a part of what's going on here is to be able to say at some point, 'OK, we can be like a base for other struggles. Maybe we will be an example for people who want a different life.'"

For another resident, if our fight against the eco-quarter "is the first struggle, then there's also the struggle for self-organization, which is already to battle against many things, ... to relearn how to take care of each other or create justice, without the institutions or justice of the state. It's an ongoing and invisible struggle. A struggle to make other spaces exist that are outside 'the norm' in a bourgeois city. Just that it exists is in itself a big struggle."

This diversity is our power but also our challenge. Our community is made up of people who come and go. It includes people who live on the land but also a diverse network of folks who don't. It makes it so hard to say where the community starts and ends. So how do we organize effectively as a community when we are not sure whether that word "community" even fits? Because the Lentillères never set out to be an intentional community, in the beginning at least.

The second value is the sense of freedom we have. There is the spatial freedom from living on what is essentially a piece of the countryside in the city. The individual gardens, each with their own style yet blending into each other, traversed by winding paths; the hidden corners; the kooky installations (like the pirate ship) and walls decorated with graffiti art; the hand-built living spaces, not beautiful exactly, but personal and often striking in some way; the cacophony of birdsong and green growth that erupts here each spring. It is *oh so* charming here—a punk version of that place with a picket fence and roses around the door, or what Hobbiton might look like if the residents were humans. And anarchists.

There is the freedom we gain from having control over this environment. We grow our own food, which brings so much joy from the direct contact we have with this land. It gives us a certain degree of food autonomy and helps us reach our "five a day." In summer, we hold a once-weekly free-price market from the produce we grow. People from the surrounding neighborhood come. Friends who make bread, herbal remedies, or jewelry join us with their things to sell too. It often makes for a soft and beautiful social moment each week, widening and broadening our sense of community. In this way we demonstrate the fertility, productivity, and value of this land. So our market is also a political statement. As one long-term resident put it, "I always feel [pride] when I see the market with all the vegetables. Wow. Lentillères. We are gardening and we have all these vegetables. And the people are coming and taking them, and are happy. Wow."

We have built up so many other resources and much infrastructure too. The machinery for farming, collective kitchen equipment, all the stuff for building and fixing bikes, and computer infrastructure. And then there are all the finds: the piles of useful junk that ebb and flow; the dumpstered food that shows up, and from time to time, forms something of a shabby free supermarket in one of the collective spaces here. There is the free shop. Then there is all the knowledge as well as skills we have amassed—to build, heal, and grow—in many different ways. It's possible to make or fix almost anything you wish to here. We share it all. It means that we rarely have to ask for anything from the world "outside." We are, to a significant degree, autonomous.

And this brings great satisfaction—satisfaction that everything here we have either built or brought back to life; that it is us who maintain it all, according to our needs and desires, with a mind toward also being the guardians of this land; that there is nobody else deciding things for us. It affords an enormous sense of purpose as well as control over our lives—a sense that anything is possible.

The long-term resident quoted above goes on to say that "I fell in love directly with this place. And that's it . . . with the garden, with what's going on here, like lots of people doing things together. I didn't know the people

at all even, 'cause I didn't speak French at that moment, . . . but just by observing them, I was thinking it was really nice. . . . I felt that it was possible
to do something here together and that the people were really open."

I ask this resident, "You're still in love with it?"

"Yes."

There is the freedom we feel to largely do as we please—a "sense of freedom in the air." It is the freedom, within limits, to express ourselves as we
wish, and the freedom afforded to us by not having to rely so much on
money—not having to work, sharing most things, producing much by ourselves, repairing everything that can be repaired, recycling, and stealing. It
means, as one resident observed, that "we live a lot in the present, in the
everyday, which takes away anxiety about what to do next, what I'm gonna
do with my life. That's a sort of liberty."

And then there's the relative freedom from oppression that many here
experience. Those of us who are not French, who are people of color, who
define ourselves as women or queer, all feel more at ease in the gardens.
Explained one person who came here as a refugee from Mali, "At the beginning I was a bit scared. I had never seen a place like this in fact. All the
gardens, the constructions. It reminded me a bit of the countryside in Africa. . . . Then I found that the people were really nice and friendly, a bit like
a big family, completely the contrary to outside, where you don't even have
the right to have a 'good morning.'" Said one person who identifies as queer,
"You do not wonder if you're a boy or you're a girl or if you're a certain race
or where you come from, so it's easier to live here than anywhere else."

Another value is the importance of collective life. Each of us gains
power by doing things together. We are able to do things we never thought
possible because of our strength in numbers. We surprise ourselves often,
in fact, with our strength. For one resident of the queer/feminist house

here, the moment when that squat was defended from police incursion was for them, and many others, an incredible instance of collective force. "The defense of La Cyprine and the opening of the house opposite it were really strong, because they were carried out by a lot of people, because they were something that we thought was not winnable, because they showed us how we could have power among many different people."

And this also frequently brings with it a lot of fun. There are many parties, concerts, shows, film screenings, and collective meals. The work we put into realizing these events (as well as the moments when we get to share them) are among the strongest in reinforcing the sense that we are together. We can feel strong because we are not alone. We are in constant contact with others, and they care for us. For one longtime resident, this is crucial, even if it isn't perfect. "I haven't made many strong friendships, but people worry about me nonetheless. I feel supported. There are some people who put their little antennas toward me to check if I am OK, and I find that cool." Many of us look for and find a sense of community here—something that meets, to some degree at least, the deep need and longing, so hard to put into words, of being held by each other, being bigger than the sum of our parts, being valuable and important to each other.

But if the extent to which we actively feel these values, or actively participate in collective or political life varies, it still amounts to a shared sense that there's so much worth defending here.

Our Decision-Making Structures

We rarely talk about these values. They are largely implied. Indeed, nothing explicit about how we see our life here together was ever written down until a year or so ago. In a way, this was deliberate and political—a desire to resist being named, overstructured, rendered powerless, and recuperated. But it also has a simple explanation. How can you say what you are when you are changing so much? And to what end? There is a fear of wrongly committing to definitions.

Our systems of decision making reflect this tension between defining and not, structuring and not. The minimal amount of collective organization is partly intentional. It is an effect of people's suspicion of overorganization; how it can make hierarchies visible but also create more hierarchies while weakening our freedom and dynamism. Then too, it shows a certain faith in the notion that structures will emerge somewhat "naturally," so we shouldn't force them. So our decision making could be considered the maximum amount of collective organization possible to maintain for an organically evolving, diverse, and constantly changing group of our size.

In the early days, there were few, if any, formal forms of collective organization. People didn't feel the need. The project was small and homogeneous enough, and the people involved were connected enough, for communication to flow more or less "freely." Yet at a certain point, the project reached a size, diversity, and complexity that necessitated more formal means of talking together: the assembly generale (general assembly, or AG) was the result. One resident who was involved in the Lentillères from the start saw the emergence of the AG as an acknowledgment that more institutionalization was inevitable as the project became more socially and practically elaborate.

"The AG didn't always exist," they noted. "We were less. At a certain point there were more inhabitants, more gardeners, and there was a point when it was necessary, even if not perfect. . . . But at a moment when there was maybe a hundred or so people using the space, the assembly was and is a way to reach some collective understandings. It excludes those who don't find meaning in it, obviously. . . . At the beginning there were less decisions to take, there was only gardening, so it was simpler. But as the society got more complex, the decisions we have to make have become more complex too."

So the monthly AG was launched as a means of structuring our discussions on things going on in and around the gardens. After awhile, however, there was resistance to this more formal way of making decisions, coming mainly from the French-born people who were part of anarchist scenes and at that time made up the majority of those involved in La Friche, or at least were the most vocal and/or influential. The result was that the AG was replaced by a monthly dinner where information could be shared. When that didn't feel adequate for the decisions at hand, the AG was reintroduced and has run continuously every month since 2015. For a period of about a year, in 2017–18, there was also a monthly assembly for the defense of the quarter, and it has recently started up again. Since 2016, there has been a monthly collective workday on the Friche as well.

Somewhat relatedly, several zines have been written about different aspects of life in the gardens, like the five-issue *Genie du lieu*, or the eight-issue *Quartier Libre*, which featured interviews with different residents and artwork about life here. Texts like these offered subjective, personal accounts of living in the Lentillères, and although they don't amount to any kind of decision-making structure per se, they have strengthened the identity of this place and influenced how people see it. So over time, the institutions of La Friche have grown, even as people have been suspicious of or nervous about them.

Our Critiques of These Structures

This minimal amount of collective organization partly explains why people were feeling like we were struggling to be a community at the time we started researching our own space. Why?

The AG is our main means of discussing things collectively. Yet it functions far from perfectly. Anywhere from between 10 and 25 percent of the people involved in La Friche typically attend. It's usually the same people—the ones who live here (as opposed to those who have their gardens here)—and thus the ones who are most active around the place. But the AG doesn't meet the needs or expectations of many others. In many cases, the points that are considered relevant to all are not necessarily those related to the concerns of everyday life here. A dispute between residents or whether the dry toilets are emptied are subjects unlikely to be on the agenda. A proposal as to whether we meet with a particular political group or plans to welcome a group from outside into our space are. The former are largely considered, or rather assumed to be, the realm of the residential collectives. In that sense, this place functions a bit like a confederation, where each individual collective has authority over the physical space it occupies and makes decisions about it independently, and where the AG exists as the overall power in decisions that impact everybody. Because "everybody" is more than just the people living here. It is also all the gardeners and supporters of La Friche as well as its residents.

What this means is, we residents have rarely, if ever, come together to talk about the issues we face just in our collective life, whether they are practical, such as our water supply or the toilets, or emotional. As a result, the focus of the AG is largely skewed toward the "properly political" struggle of the Lentillères. The AG, in this way, unintentionally reinforces a certain hierarchy of concerns, where everyday issues are subsumed by supposedly higher political ones. As such, there are those who feel that the content of the AG is often largely irrelevant to their daily lives. One resident, who originally comes from sub-Saharan Africa, observed, "I don't go all the time, 'cause when I do, I can't follow all the points. It's not clear, and they talk about things that aren't important to living here."

Then there are those who feel that the discussions are hard to follow because they depend on a higher level of French comprehension than many have. As one resident from Mali put it, themselves a fluent French speaker, "There are people who have things to say, but they cannot speak French well, so they feel bad" about talking in the AGs. Speakers for whom French is their first language recognize this as a problem. One native French speaker expressed this issue: "A structure of domination that's strong is language, that we use French, and many people aren't comfortable with French and are quickly excluded." Moreover, the language is often specific to the anarchist counterculture and thus somehow technical, which for one native French resident, was a barrier to their participation. "And it's not just for francophone speakers; there are plenty of codes and rules, which are written nowhere—words that are not necessarily academic but are still inaccessible to people who are not part of their milieu. It's classist too, so class relations remain unchallenged and reinforced."

Whether language is actually a structure of domination here or an individual barrier that we have yet to overcome, we have frequently tried to tackle the question. We have often used translation during meetings—whether this has involved announcing meetings ahead of time in multiple languages, offering direct translation during them, or providing other means to communicate, such as opportunities to submit ideas before or after meetings—but this has rarely worked to diversify who attends, perhaps because it doesn't overcome a certain barrier of detachment from the conversation. Speaking French badly still means having a limited ability to get caught up in the debate, in the moment.

It also means that our collective structures are dominated by certain people: those for whom French is their first tongue, those most familiar with a certain way of doing politics, or the ones who have been here the longest and are the most highly educated. This point is not lost on those who fit this description. "Me, for example, I feel like I'm dominant in the sense that I'm male, highly educated, older, and have been here a long time," said one resident. "But sometimes I feel people don't feel I'm conscious of these things, when actually I am quite conscious of my privileges." At the same time, these dominant social positions affect and/or afflict those who fit within them. Remarked another resident, "The AG is a good example of how domination is exercised here. It's a clear tool of decision making, but there is a tacit way of behaving and participating in it, and there's a fear of judgment for me in not being able to participate correctly."

It is overly simplistic to say that it's a case of structures of domination—being white, a cis man, and/or strong bodied, for example—playing themselves out here. But these social codes go unsaid, and as such, create anxiety over how we meet a standard of behavior that we are not really sure is there. It creates inhibitions and self-policing. As a newer resident, who comes originally from Mali, states, "I went sometimes, but I didn't speak. I didn't know what to say."

Many ascribe the reason why not everybody attends meetings to the fact that we came to live here in different ways, with different intentions. There are those who came here for explicitly political reasons, and there are those who came here out of a clear and practical need. Meetings seem to work better for the former than the latter, and equally reflect this interest in so-called political rather than everyday concerns. Ultimately those who do participate in the political life of this place see that there are indeed structures that exclude people, but the overriding suspicion remains that the main reason is a lack of interest in collective life, or collective life with us. After all, there is nothing here that forces people to participate. So another factor that creates a hierarchy in who makes decisions is the fact that there are some who have chosen to devote their lives to participating in building collective structures in this place. These differing levels of commitment are the hardest form of hierarchy to tackle because you can't demand the same level of engagement from everyone who lives here. "Not everyone can or wants to come," commented a resident, "and yet the decisions of the assembly impact them. We haven't found a solution to that."

Those who don't go to meetings, however, often feel that the AG doesn't represent them. What they see as being valued or considered as collective life within the AG is not actually relevant to them, and what they do consider important is somehow devalued, ignored, or not heard. This is different from an out-and-out disinterest in collective life per se on the part of those who don't attend. We assume within the whole project that we have the same views as to what counts as a life in common, when in actuality, perhaps we have different perspectives on what matters. That's something we have never discussed either.

The AG and other meetings form the visible part of our decision-making structure. There are numerous invisible, informal, and less intentionally organized ways, though, that people make decisions here. These ways work largely through affinity, meaning that they function between friends and/or those who trust each other, and happen largely by accident or in social settings rather than in formal meetings. For one resident, this informality is also quite fruitful and necessary. "To the side of the meetings, all the time on the paths, to the left and right, there's a sharing of informa-tion. It's informal, but it's a decision-making structure nonetheless in my opinion. Crossing people in the garden, having a coffee together, having breakfast together—there is always something to discuss."

Of course, structures like these are not freely accessible to everybody. Affinity functions through trust, which is something that people build be-tween themselves over time and protects us. At the same time, it functions through popularity, or on one's ability to follow the invisible rules and social codes (which in our milieu, means dressing in a way that is scruffy yet prac-tical; speaking in the right tone; being polite but not overly so; listening and not interrupting; being funny or lighthearted; being sociable in general as well as pleasant; and enjoying parties and alcohol). As such, affinity or trust is only available to certain people.

The classic text "The Tyranny of Structureless" by feminist Jo Freeman talks about how groups that lack formal structures for decision making do not in fact have no structure at all. Rather, they are groups where informal, unnamed, and invisible structures come to thrive in their place. These in-visible structures often function through social codes. Furthermore, in such a situation where friendship and political activity come together, what fre-quently results is an elite within the group, constituted by those who can perform these social codes the best, and who are strongly connected to each other and can reinforce each other's point of view. As opposed to cre-ating horizontality, power becomes concentrated among a few, strength-ening certain hierarchies. In a situation like ours, with a minimal level of structure, this has indeed been the case. It has meant that many people who do not consider themselves part of the more anarchistic tendencies that are dominant in this place now (for instance, those who were originally part of this project from the more leftist and citizens' groups) have felt over-looked and pushed out.

250

KING

As one person put it, "It's hard to find your way in here if you don't already have affinity with people. Affinity is good in that it gives [one] confidence, but bad in that it excludes. You can't welcome everyone." Commented another, "All these codes makes a barrier that's impossible to cross, that's impermeable from the outside. La Ferme, Cappuccino, and La Jungla are all examples of groups that came and weren't included.[3] La Jungla is an example of a group that resisted this process that makes it so hard to enter. . . . But how many people broke their teeth against this wall in the process? People work hard to get included, and many people fail."

These informal structures exist within formal structures too, because those social codes function there. Again, those who aren't so good at performing these codes feel and/or are marginalized. "It creates a situation," noted one resident, "where the influential people are simply replaced by other influential people rather than that we manage to overcome hierarchy."

To have affinity among all in a diverse community that sees a fair amount of coming and going among the population is extremely difficult. What results is a certain trust deficit, which means that meetings are often either superficial or else long as we attempt to find that trust, thereby further excluding certain folks. For a member of the Tuareg community who lives

---

3. La Ferme is the name of a house that was the first building to be occupied on La Friche, and over the years, has been occupied by many different collectives. Last year, for instance, a group of students lived there. Their initial connection to the Lentillères was via a squatted cantine, in which they created a collective kitchen project together. By the end of last year, however, after several conflicts, all of them had left. La Junga is a housing collective that started in 2015. It was initially met with hostility. Not aware of any collective process of how a group might stay here, La Junga moved in with several caravans and installed itself on land reserved for gardening. People were upset that La Junga didn't consult anyone.

here, the lengthy meetings are a major barrier. "One thing I don't like here are the long meetings. They can make a meeting like a day. I don't have the patience to stay all day. In our place, we never make meetings. If we want to speak, we just speak like ten minutes or something like that. Me, I'm staying like one hour. After that, I will leave." They also noted that they "understand why they have to make the meetings long, because everybody has their own idea." Among the Tuareg, "if someone makes a decision and 40 percent of this decision I don't agree with, and 60 percent I can agree with, I can forget the 40 percent. Everybody is like that. But here [among the Lentillères in general], if someone makes a decision, there is a lot who can say 'no, no, no.' For us, if someone makes a decision, we can agree with it. But if someone wants to make a decision here, it is complicated."

The Tuareg, who don't make up a homogeneous group, but did largely come here and organize together within the Lentillères, are a cohesive and tight-knit community within the gardens. They pray together five times a day, for example, and have the chance to express their views at the end of the last prayer sitting each evening. There is a lot of trust among them, so there is no need to work out all the finer details of every decision. They can assume things, which is not possible in the wider community of this place.

What this all adds up to is differences in our levels of inclusion or exclusion, the degree to which we identify with the collective or feel alone in it, and the extent to which we feel committed to or responsible for the Lentillères.

Another person with the Tuareg community, although they feel quite happy to let others make decisions for them, explained that they "don't feel exactly like I have a responsibility to this place. I am staying with these people, but I leave the responsibilities for the others. I am just a neighbor here. I live here, but I cannot say this is my place. . . . You [have to take] care about the place, but you can't say this place is for me; that means I am not the owner of the place."

It means that making good decisions together—by which we mean decisions where it feels like everybody had a say, and where the process and outcome are ones that people can trust—is rare and difficult. We are affected by the limited structures we have in place, and the sense that only a certain proportion of the people involved here feel at ease enough, included enough, representative enough, or powerful enough to actually deliberate about and make decisions in our public sphere or in private.

For some, it means that our decision making is so compromised as to barely exist or, at least, count for something. One resident observed, "We rarely manage to make decisions. ... The biggest decision, to exclude people, was actually taken by a few and then given a sheen of democracy by inviting others to a meeting about it, where they agreed. Decisions are always taken before or after the meeting. It's always like that."

Back to Last Summer

And so when we arrived in summer 2018 at what was a crisis, we were already suffering the effects of a long-standing, compromised decision-making structure. The end of the summer was a particularly useful moment to tackle this because it is also a time when actions are relaunched again, after the summer "break." But it was a moment of necessity too. There was the feeling that our decision-making structures were letting us down more so than ever; that too many assumptions had been allowed to build up. As one person put it, "It's not an issue of only one subject but instead many different subjects," adding that there were likely many more concerns "than just the stories from the last year."

This was particularly so for several reasons. Many new residents had come to live here during that last year, meaning that our community had swelled—doubled—in a short span of time. Many of the new residents came from the Tuareg community, and although collective life among them is strong, it was a different kind and separate from the one already here. It was perhaps unclear to the Tuareg how to engage in the collective life of the Lentillères and make a contribution, or something they didn't desire in the same way as we were doing it.

The Tuareg had come to the Lentillères after a collective attempt to open a squat in the city had failed. They were instead welcomed into various collectives within the gardens. When any large group of people join another group, that integration can be difficult, both practically and emotionally (this was an influx of almost a fifth of the existing population of La Friche at that time). Over time, some of the people were more integrated into the collectives than others. Among some in the gardens, the disparity in living conditions (the amount of available living space, participation in collective daily life, or access to resources) between us older residents and our new neighbors suggested that some collectives were actually resistant to welcoming them in. This became an especially strong critique among those who felt that they had integrated with the Tuareg in more meaningful ways. In practice, this meant that many of the Tuareg were marginalized in terms of access to space and resources. Many of them also struggled to engage in collective life here. For some non-Tuareg residents, this appeared as if the Tuareg didn't care about collective life or even didn't respect it. None of this was said in public, but resentments built up, and partly as a result, people neglected to care for the collective spaces in the gardens, and so they deteriorated.

Add to this the fact that earlier in the summer, as already mentioned,

---

some traumatic events had taken place in the gardens—followed by the expectation that we should come to some decisions about them, but where we repeatedly failed to do so. There was a feeling that events had run too fast, that we couldn't keep up with understanding or comprehending all the details, and couldn't take the time to come to any conclusions. The result was a sense of failure and being let down by each other. Accusations of racism started to emerge, and conflicts took place. There was an urgent need to try something else in terms of how we work and find a new form in which to create more space to express our feelings, instead of among informal circles of affinity.

The meeting in the pirate ship was organized differently from the AG. People were invited in advance to submit their ideas on the topics at hand as a means of opening a space to those who didn't feel OK about speaking up in meetings, for whatever reason. Those topics related directly to everyday life. Facilitators were carefully chosen and took the role seriously. There was a strong feeling of relevance. That so many people came to the meetings also demonstrated our commitment to each other and the issues facing us.

Following the meeting at the pirate ship, there were two more meetings, and there was an attempt to use different ways to diffuse the tension and really reflect on the racism accusation. But despite these efforts, our discussions remained aggressive and accusatory. People took sides, between a small group of people who accused everyone else, and the rest who felt more and more united in light of this seeming attack. Despite dominating the floor in both meetings, the small group declared that no one was willing to hear its critique. The group's members threatened to destroy this place. In both cases, they stormed out, and left everyone else, stunned, still committed to scrutinizing the ways that racism exists here, yet with no way of knowing how to do that. Exhaustion and a lack of faith set in. More weeks passed, and the group of accusers started threatening and intimidating different people living here. After a meeting to decide what to do about it, this group was asked to leave.

Many were left feeling confused by this series of jolting events and uncomfortable with the decision to exclude people, but also convinced that there was nothing else to do than take this emergency action. As one person commented, "It was really hard, but we tried and we talk a lot about it, so for me it was something—I could not say nice, but something good that we tried to solve this, and we talked a lot and we tried to learn more. We tried to know each other better, to do better. . . . This was good for me in this case, but I can't say I think I was proud. Also, I can say I was ashamed. It was really difficult."

Observed another, "It was not a discussion that led to something, but the process—taking time to talk in different languages about difficult subjects—it is not exemplary, and we must be careful if we quote it [as such], because it was an exceptional moment, and it was the case that people who did not identify with 'us' had pointed this subject out. But the process it created was a powerful one."

Many have been left with the feeling that things are still unfinished, and that maybe the time is ripe to start talking about these things again, yet that remains to be seen.

And Beyond

Fast-forward a few more months. The dull gray of winter has again been replaced with the bright heat of an early spring. It is April 9, 2019, and our spring party is in full swing: three days and nights of concerts, workshops, collective meals, and an open door to the rest of Dijon. The tool shed has become a temporary home for a live radio broadcast, the concert space is decorated with bunting, the outside bar is busy, and there is an acoustic concert taking place in the Tuareg tea tent. People are slowly filtering into the Lentillères, returning from the city following a Critical Mass bike ride. It has taken months of preparation to get here—many meetings, online discussions, postering, and flyering—and a week of hard labor to put all the infrastructure in place to welcome the hundreds of visitors who will pass through our squatted land this weekend. There is a strong sense among us that we are a "we" at this moment. And we are here again, together, still. Tired and happy. That sense of togetherness is pervasive and strong. The events of last summer feel far away, and we are reminded again why we are here.

*

Natasha King is a resident of the Lentillères. She has written for publications such as *Aeon* and *Roar* magazines. Her latest book, *No Borders: The Politics of Immigration Control and Resistance* (Zed, 2016), was included on Verso's top five essential reading list on the changing role of borders. Natasha would like to thank all the people, her neighbors, who took the time to speak with her. It was, in the end, a fascinating, cathartic, and as always imperfect form of collective work. Thanks also to those who took the time to read and comment on previous drafts. Special thanks to Paloma for her insightful analysis and help in conducting these interviews.

Cindy Milstein

CODA: WAKING TO REVOLUTION

My alarm and cell phone conspired that morning.
Both startled me from sleep at once.
"8 a.m.!" chimed my clock.
"Mubarak stepped down!" declared a text message.[1]

I nearly always get up at eight, here in San Francisco.
But I've never woken to a revolution before.

In faraway Egypt, liberation had been squared in Cairo's Tahrir.
A thirty-year dictatorship was toppled.
As a friend later quipped, the strategy for success is: don't leave.
Occupy a key spot, by the millions, and don't leave.

Yet the victory was not simply due to sheer numbers.
Nor was it the result of occupation alone.
The triumph resided in the constitution of a self-managed commons.
In the almost-mundane fact of that community's working existence.

---

1. I originally wrote this piece as my part of a picture-essay in Cindy Milstein and Erik Ruin, *Paths toward Utopia: Graphic Explorations of Everyday Anarchism* (Oakland, CA: PM Press, 2012), 86–102. Inspired by the 2011 revolution in Egypt centered on Tahir Square, it was published before the full weight of the brutal and deadly suppression was evident.

For eighteen days, people enacted—and reveled in—their own *power*.

I've long believed that self-organization works—better than any other form.
That people, all of us, can and want to self-determine.
That we can and want to self-govern, guided by dignity and even love.
But what I realized that morning was, deep down, I had also come not to
   believe it.

Since utopian notions are negated by almost everything today,
I had unconsciously lost that trust.

The uprising began with a surprise.
As if from nowhere, overnight, people discovered their collective
   strength.
A euphoric self-confidence took hold.
This jolted other people—like me—to recall that possibility begets
   possibility.

Those of us who are heretics are also archaeologists.
We sift through the shards of past experiments,
Buried in the rich subterranean,
For evidence of what Hannah Arendt called "the lost treasure" of
   revolutions,
The "organizational impulses of the people themselves":
Councils, militias, confederations, soviets, consultas, assemblies . . .
The infinite lived innovations in bottom-up social relations.
We string these gems together,
Tossing them in the air, as new celestial bodies to guide others.

In Cairo, from these glittering scraps,
People built their own city in a square, rapidly, without leaders.
An impromptu prism,
Affording partial answers to the loftiest and lowliest of questions:
"How can we transform gender relations?"
"In the absence of coercion, who will take out the trash?"

That morning, when Mubarak fell, my mind was flooded with images,
Gleaned from the eyewitness accounts I'd hungrily read,
Of *how* people crafted their autonomous society,
Out of necessity and under sometimes-deadly adversity.

Of how people protected each other:
The makeshift helmets, from buckets and bottles, saucepans and foam.
The self-defense committees, and their temporary barricades and
    checkpoints.
Whistling as a signal when assistance was needed,
Or people sleeping and sitting on tanks, to neutralize them as weapons.

Of how people cared for each other:
The clinics and pharmacies, in alleyways and a now-former fast-food
    spot,
Where volunteer doctors in white coats freely dispensed medical aid.
Or the pop-up kindergartens,
So families and children could protest—and play.

Of how people provided for each other:
The communal kitchens that also served as skill shares,

In which each volunteer would show the next person what to do before
  leaving.
The daily arrival of tents and blankets, and newspapers publicly posted.
Almost everything for everyone, free.

Of how people organized with each other:
A young woman made a video, others wrote handbills,
And from twenty-one decentralized spots, people initially converged on
  the square.
Neighborhood assemblies arose for decisions,
While committees invented systems for garbage collection, recycling,
  and cleanup.
People devised a public sphere of indie media, speakers' areas, and art,
Along with martyrs' walls to remember those killed in this battle.

The afternoon of that morning when Mubarak was deposed,
I went to a solidarity celebration in San Francisco.
"Can you believe it?" said an Egyptian emigrant,
Fresh from another celebration at his mosque.

We'd never met.
He introduced me to his family here,
Explained that he'd been in constant touch with relatives in Tahrir,
And for an hour, told me about all that had changed.

"My people did it themselves, sharing all."
"Muslims and Christians were united."
"Women were equal participants, and sexual harassment seemed to
  disappear."

His four daughters, all under ten years old, smiled up at me.
"It was never like that before."

Nothing lasts.
Relationships end.
Friends die.
Even capitalism will be history someday.

It's what we do to reawaken each other that matters,
Breathing life into self-organization, the working actuality of freedom.

That's the victory, the revolution,
The truth of our power:
That we know how to create lives worth living.
Knowing that such moments, too, won't last.

Yet afterward, when the squares and capitols are forcibly emptied,
The world never fully goes back to normal.
We aren't the same people.
Some of our experimentation sticks,
Making us a little less estranged, a little more heartened.

Even when presidents and property, police and prisons, crushingly return,
Memory, like some scrappy carrier pigeon, transports our courage,
Upward, to the next rebel commune,
So the next time, and the time after that,
And perhaps even now,
We'll know how to do-it-ourselves even more beautifully.

ACKNOWLEDGMENTS

When Andrew Zonneveld with AK Press first approached me about doing this anthology, he wanted me to gather all of Murray Bookchin's writings on direct democracy in one place. I'd already done most of that work years ago for a spiral-bound "reader" that I'd made and photocopied in limited quantity for my "direct democracy" sessions at the monthlong anarchist summer school known as the Institute for Social Ecology in Plainfield, Vermont. That collection showed how Murray's notions of politics unfolded during his many years of organizing and writing, remaining dynamic and, I would argue, radical. I couldn't get copyright permission to turn those essays into a book, but that bump in the road completely transformed this project, and for the better, including because Andrew hung in with me on reimagining its shape and scope.

Rather than centering on one person's view, however elastic, *Deciding for Ourselves* illustrates that people can engage in forms of self-governance that make sense for their own circumstances, all the while holding onto liberatory sensibilities. It is, in part, an answer to Murray's critics, who've alleged that direct democracy is flawed in that it's only applicable to limited types of people or locales. Equally, it's partly a corrective to Murray's own inability to see certain peoples or places as revolutionary sites. But more than anything, it is a homage to Murray's impact on my own and so many others' anarchism—emphasizing not only an antagonism toward the state but also prefigurative forms of decision making outside statist logics. So I want to acknowledge, with deep affection, that Murray's thinking haunts these pages, in the best of spirits.

Once this project steered toward contemporary spaces of actually existing self-governance, I needed to go on a scouting mission for writers. What you won't see on these pages are all the many detours and dead-ends. What you will see are the essays that each contributor gave so much of themselves to make happen, precisely because of their own commitment to the politics embodied in this collection. I am grateful to all the voices in this anthology, whether quoted, interviewed, or the author. In particular, I offer deep appreciation to all the writers; they let me edit and edit and edit their pieces with such grace, patience, and good cheer. It was a true pleasure and honor to curate this container, an edited anthology, for their powerful stories.

I also want to thank all those people who generously offered me leads, contacts, and advice during my scouting trip for writers and information, including (but likely not limited to): Bradley, Gabriel Kuhn, Pavlos Stavropoulos, daph ben david, Rushdia Mehreen, Pascale Brunet, Darian Razdar, Shiri Pasternak, Rebecca Winter, Paloma Soledad Contreras, Mette Morgenstjerne, Bruno Renero-Hannan, Andalusia Knoll Soloff, Martha Pskowski, Andréa Schmidt, John Jordan, Jerome Roos, Joris Leverink, nico, cixy, mixtec, nata, noresil, Paloma, Dawn Paley, Black Rose / Rosa Negra Anarchist Federation, Bree, Sofía, Karla Tait, Anne Spice, Freda Huson, Denise Cole, Dianne Rochleau, Nathaniel Miller, Bianca Shana'a, Jonny Leavitt, Rona Lorimer, Andy Cornell, and anyone who shared my social media "ask" for contributor suggestions.

I extend my appreciation, too, to those authors who agreed to support this book with a blurb, knowing how much effort those few lines take to craft: William C. Anderson, Carla Bergman, Roxanne Dunbar-Ortiz, Madeline ffitch, Matt Hern, and Dean Spade. A big thank you as well to Dawn Finley, Madeleine Nerenberg, and Courtney Remacle for their editing aid on my own piece for this anthology—especially at the last minute. I also continue to be glad that AK Press exists in a world that isn't kind to anarchist publishers, and that the collective believes in and supports my projects by putting them into print. Thank you, Andrew, Zach Blue, Charles Weigl, and the other members of AK Press.

I am honored that Jeff Clark—under the studio name Crisis—is my accomplice on yet another anthology, bringing his keen graphic design sensibilities, par excellence, to *Deciding for Ourselves* as a labor of love and friendship. His striking, sophisticated, and yet open look for this book, coupled the contributors' words, makes for promise-filled beauty indeed!

And even though neither was directly part of this collection, I want to give a shout-out to my chosen sisters, Karen Milstein and Laura MacDonald; they never fail to remind me that abiding love and care are not only possible in theory but also doable in practice.

Last but not least, I want to recognize all the pain, loss, and grief that goes into carving out and sustaining spaces of "deciding for ourselves." Such sorrows, alas, often seem to be all that outlives those places when they are crushed by forces that want to decide for us, against us. It has been difficult, emotionally, to see this book to completion while police, militaries, heads of state, and other institutions of violence are busy trying to annihilate some of the spaces so magically explored in this anthology. But it is incomparably more difficult to know that people are risking their lives to defend the collective freedom that they themselves have built, and are being made to suffer mightily for it. That is all the more reason we need to keep alive the joys that are present in such experiments too, and remember that there's a thread of dignity and solidarity that connects them all. As scholar Saidiya Hartman observed in her book *Lose Your Mother*, "Must the story of the defeated always be a story of defeat? Is it too late to imagine that their lives might be redeemed or to fashion an antidote to oblivion? Is it too late to believe their struggles cast a shadow into a future in which they might finally win?"[1] Even as we need to mourn our dead, we equally need to continue to mend the world for the living.

—Cindy Milstein, December 2019

---

1. Saidiya Hartman, *Lose Your Mother: A Journey along the Atlantic Slave Route* (New York: Farrar, Straus and Giroux, 2007), 192.

AK PRESS is small, in terms of staff and resources, but we also manage to be one of the world's most productive anarchist publishing houses. We publish close to twenty books every year, and distribute thousands of other titles published by like-minded independent presses and projects from around the globe. We're entirely worker run and democratically managed. We operate without a corporate structure—no boss, no managers, no bullshit.

The Friends of AK program is a way you can directly contribute to the continued existence of AK Press, and ensure that we're able to keep publishing books like this one! Friends pay $25 a month directly into our publishing account ($30 for Canada, $35 for international), and receive a copy of every book AK Press publishes for the duration of their membership! Friends also receive a discount on anything they order from our website or buy at a table: 50 percent on AK titles, and 20 percent on everything else. We have a Friends of AK e-book program as well: $15 a month gets you an electronic copy of every book we publish for the duration of your membership. You can even sponsor a deeply discounted membership for someone in prison.

E-mail friendsofak@akpress.org for more info, or visit the Friends of AK Press website: akpress.org/friends.html.

There are always great book projects in the works—so sign up now to become a Friend of AK Press, and let the presses roll!